Comments of Readers

In this well written, well organized study, Brian Russell sets contemporary worship in historical context, makes a case for utilizing it and offers a step-by-step process for shaping it within 21st century "mainline" congregations. The breadth of Russell's work is impressive, and his theological insights make the book a valuable guide for clergy and laity alike.

— Rev. Dr. Bill J. Leonard
James and Marilyn Dunn Professor of Baptist Studies
and Church History, Wake Forest University

Brian Russell's book is a great resource for churches considering starting a contemporary worship service, are seeking to reinvigorate their existing contemporary services, or want to explore the role of music, traditional or contemporary, in the life of worship. Brian's book does a wonderful job of validating and advocating for both traditional and contemporary music in worship.

Mr. Russell advocates for effective sacred music in every setting, as long as it is relevant to the people hearing it. He provides clear, experienced strategies for how to develop effective sacred music programs for contemporary worship.

— Dr. Danny Frye, Director
Instrumental Studies, High Point University

For any pastors or worship leaders interested in either starting a contemporary worship service or bringing new life to an existing service, *The Contemporary Worship Handbook* is a must read. From the nuts and bolts of hiring effective leaders, assembling a praise team and music selection, to naming a service (or not naming it), budgets and marketing strategies, Brian has covered them all. Brian reminds us, as worship leaders, that we must continually ask ourselves if our worship is helping our congregations experience God. Isn't that our goal? This book helps us all get there.

— Rev. Peggy A. Finch
Memorial United Methodist Church

Twenty-five years ago I attended church conferences that clearly articulated what was coming and what was at stake: "Lead worship that is accessible, engaging and relevant, that resonates with your congregation's theology, mission and vision...or you will decline rapidly in the 21st century."

In 1997 I accepted a call to a congregation I'm still serving that gave me primary responsibility for a new worship service. After several years of success and struggles, we realized we needed a musician who shared the vision, who also possessed the theological bent, leadership skills and courageous passion to explore and eventually lead this journey. Brian Russell is that person. This book is the result of a challenging, grace-filled adventure that continues to evolve beyond his years with us. I know from experience that Brian's guidance in this book will give your congregation the opportunity to design and lead vibrant worship, and I commend it to you with confidence and joy.

— Rev. Jay Hilbinger, Senior Pastor
First Lutheran Church
Greensboro, North Carolina

The Complete
Contemporary Worship
Handbook

The Complete
Contemporary
Worship
Handbook

How to Build and Sustain Meaningful Worship
in Modern Denominational Churches

BY BRIAN T. RUSSELL

LANGMARC
PUBLISHING

Austin, Texas

The Complete Contemporary Worship Handbook

How to Build and Sustain Meaningful Worship in Modern Denominational Churches

By Brian T. Russell

Cover layout: Michael Qualben
Cover artist © 2016 Lynda Hepler

Published by LangMarc Publishing
P.O. Box 90488
Austin, TX 78709
www.langmarc.com

Library of Congress Control Number: 2016954362
ISBN: 978-1-880292-06-8

Dedication

For my dad
who traded his car for a guitar,
an amp and a drum set
so my brother and I could make some noise.
Thanks, Pop.
And for my mom
who always saw
the art in me, even when
I did not.

Table of Contents

Section 22: Reclaiming the "E" Word

Foreword

How can we re-energize our worship services? What can we do to make our worship inviting to more people? How can we design worship that touches all of our people when stylistic and musical preferences vary so much from one person to another? We need a new sound system for our sanctuary but we don't have much money; what do you recommend we do? These are questions pastoral leaders, congregants and students ask me when they learn that I am a professor of worship.

The questions are not surprising. After all, weekly worship is the focal point of most congregations' ministries. Worship draws people from their homes and jobs, from their everyday lives, to sing and pray in community for an hour or so. Worship offers people sacred time and space where they can rest their deepest joys and sorrows in the grace of God. Worship sparks worshipers' spiritual imaginations, stirs their hearts toward the presence and promises of God, stimulates their minds to think anew about theological matters, and sends them out to embody in their work and play God's good Gospel news.

At least, worship *can* do all of these things. Worship can also at times struggle to find its identity and vitality as congregations wrestle with declining membership, concerns about finances, and changing cultural attitudes about the role of churches in neighborhoods and communities.

In these pages, Brian Russell offers to congregations whose worship is thriving and to congregations who seek worship renewal wisdom for designing meaningful contemporary services that enliven worshipers' encounters with God. Well-researched and accessible to a range of worshipers and worship leaders, this book invites readers to lean in and listen with generous and curious ears to the lively soundscapes of Christian worship today. What readers hear as they journey that soundscape with Russell, and what they can imagine as a result of the journey, are possibilities for revitalizing worship.

A great gift of this book is Russell's voice as guide. Russell writes in a conversational way about what he has learned from his diverse experiences as worship designer and leader. His seasoned passion for worship that transforms is a bright thread that weaves together the multiple pieces of the book.

The multiple pieces of the book are also gifts to readers. Leading readers through topics ranging from historical and theological topographies of worship to the nuts and bolts of bulletins and budgets, microphones and sound systems, Russell achieves his dual goals of helping worship leaders to explore contemporary worship on "macro and micro levels" and providing congregations with a "catalyst" to start substantive and much-needed conversations about worship.

I celebrate that Russell said "yes" to the people who told him to "write this stuff down." He has found a way to organize in handbook form what worship leaders too often carry in their hearts, minds, and bodies as tacit knowledge. Worship leaders just do what they do. Russell has put on paper what he has learned about what he does. In this book, he describes why and how he does what he does. He offers his tacit knowledge as practical and theological wisdom. Now, when people ask me questions about how to renew worship in their congregations, I can point them to an experienced and creative conversation partner whose written-down wisdom about worship will inform and inspire.

Rev. Jill Crainshaw, Ph.D.
Wake Forest University Divinity School
Winston-Salem, NC:

Preface

Notes on how to use this book: In early 2014, I attended the "Frames" seminar series hosted by the Barna Group.[1] This organization, through extensive demographic research, has come to the conclusion that people in North America are reading very differently now than we did in past generations. They found we are reading significantly more words each day but in smaller amounts or sessions. We are all living in the screenage.

Millennials especially are moving away from reading two hundred-page books in their entirety. Many of us have a stack of books, all with bookmarks sticking out of the sides. Since reading an entire book has become impractical for many of us, information needs to be more streamlined. As North American culture grows increasingly kinesthetic, the information in the books we write needs to be more compartmentalized. We want readers to be able to quickly access information and then come back to it as needed.

In an effort to present the information in this book in a way that is accessible to our changing reading habits, I divided the book into 22 major sections. Within those major sections there are a number of topics each with individual headers. Each topic is designed to function on its own and not necessarily be dependent on other sections of the book in order to have meaning. Readers who want to read this book cover to cover may find that certain points will be repeated, as they may be germane to a particular topic. As you peruse the table of contents, my hope is you can go directly to the topics most applicable to your work and interests.

I have written this book to function like an owners' manual, dealing with contemporary worship on micro and macro levels. My goal is to provide an accessible resource that is informative, thought provoking and useful to anyone working with contemporary worship. If my vision for this book is realized, many of you will critically consume this work, accepting parts of it, questioning others, and allowing it to be a catalyst for meaningful conversations in your faith communities.

Acknowledgements

I thank my beautiful and talented wife Elizabeth. Her inexhaustible work ethic and relentless encouragement has freed and empowered me to complete this book. I am in awe of her accomplishments and hope that this work honors her investment in me.

A huge thank you to Susan Klaiber for seeing something in me, taking me out from hiding, for helping me find my gifts and giving me an opportunity to share them.

Thanks to Drs. Bill Leonard, Jill Crainshaw and to Jeremy Begbie for taking time from their schedules to contribute to this book. Rubbing shoulders with these great thinkers was a particular joy for me.

Thank you, Rev. Charlie Zimmerman, for giving me inspiration and a formative nudge to get started.

Thank you to Rev. Ben Devoid and Rev. Peggy Finch for your trust, support, inspiration and example of ambitious leadership.

In many ways, this book is a dedication to my dear friends and Moravian kin – Phillip Pfeiffer and Cindy Good. They walked this journey with me and taught me about goodness, grace and friendship as we studied how to move the Gospel forward. Both left us too soon, and I hope that this book honors their memory.

Finally, thanks to Rev. Jay Hilbinger for being my spiritual brother, teammate and war buddy as we learned together how to establish and maintain contemporary worship.

Introduction

I'm not cool. I'm not a hipster with a waxed mustache and a ukulele. I do have black plastic-framed glasses, which I fished out of the bargain bin about seven years before they came into vogue. I'm not a rock star. No one wants my autograph. Also, I'm not smarter than you. I don't live in an ivory tower. I'm educated and intellectual, but I am comfortably average as compared to my academic peers. Who I am is a Christian who has dedicated his life and career to developing and maintaining contemporary worship in denominational settings. I write from real experience with real churches with real challenges and, thankfully, real success stories.

Over the past 13 years, I've become a student of contemporary worship, learning from worship leaders around the country, from great minds at hallowed universities and from my own trial and error. I hope to combine this research into a resource that informs, equips and motivates worship leaders in a practical way.

Why did I write this book? For the same reason that anyone does anything in church: because someone asked me to. After serving as director of contemporary worship in a Lutheran church for a few years, we started seeing tremendous growth. Our church became known as a model for effective contemporary worship. I received calls from other churches, soliciting advice and scheduling visits. I had ministerial "street-cred." As I was giving these other churches advice, I thought, "I should write this stuff down."

While on a retreat for pastors and ordination candidates, I found myself in several conversations with pastors who were looking to start or redirect contemporary worship at their churches. My advice to them was well received. One of those pastors said, "You really should write a book!"

A few years back I was having lunch with my pastor, who had recently retired from parish ministry and was working as a congregational coach for the North Carolina Synod. We talked about congregations that were struggling with contemporary worship. I told him I would be available if he needed some help with any of them and gave him some initial advice to pass along. He said, "You really should write this stuff down." We talked about how a practical book on the subject of contemporary worship could be very useful to these congregations.

As much as I resisted making the commitment to write a book, struggling with fears that I'm not smart enough, famous enough or hip enough, it became apparent that I have a strange and unique calling to do so.

Back in the late 1990's when I started serving in contemporary worship, the only book I could find on the subject was Rory Noland's terrific work called *Heart of the Artist*. Noland does a great job preparing those of us who lead music in worship to deal with the challenges and rewards of this type of ministry. I think that for any bookshelf my book winds up on, it would be good to have Noland's book as well. When I first read Noland's book, I learned valuable lessons that have shaped my approach to worship leadership.[2] But as much as I love *Heart of the Artist*, it is dated as a resource for modern worship leaders and is not particularly geared toward contemporary worship.

Beyond Noland, there is a dramatic lack of books that inform the work of creating contemporary worship. A search for "contemporary worship" in the Wake Forest University library databases reveals several articles but surprisingly few results for books on the subject. I found one book written in 1997 on contemporary worship, two from the 1970s and an academic study published in 2007, but it was difficult to find a current, useful book on contemporary worship. A search of the Barnes and Noble's retail database yielded just seven results for the phrase "contemporary worship," none of which were current. The need for such a resource exists, and I am inspired to produce this book as a way of addressing that need.

It is my goal and my hope that anyone who reads this book will find it well worth their time and that anyone who purchases it will feel they've gotten their money's worth. With this work, I do not intend to draw conclusions but rather start conversations.

Much of the content of this book is drawn from my own experience, which means that a good bit is editorial. My intention is to offer the wisdom I have gained through trial and error. My experience comes from a time of transition in the 21st century North American Christian denominational landscape. Specifically, my experience comes from working in Lutheran, Methodist, Baptist and Catholic churches. I pray that worship leaders in any denominational (or nondenominational) setting will find value in this content.

Section 1

What is Contemporary Worship?
A Musician's Point of View

1. Definition

2. Music is Important

3. Music Lasts

4. Music: A Tool to Discover Theology

1. Definition

Contemporary worship in a denominational setting is defined and understood by its juxtaposition to traditional worship. When we offer contemporary worship at a church that also has traditional worship, it becomes part of a liturgical portfolio, allowing for specialization. I am writing this book as a contemporary worship director, but I don't want anyone to assume I've concluded that traditional worship is any less valuable than contemporary. I will say that contemporary music, because of its inherent longing to reflect its context both culturally and socially, has a vast potential for reaching new members. Contemporary worship broadens our opportunities and gives us a wider pallet to work with as we endeavor to bring life to worship and to animate Scripture. Contemporary worship by my definition, however, doesn't exist without traditional worship.

Contemporary worship is distinguished from traditional by an approachable liturgy, a relaxed atmosphere and music that is influenced by popular culture. Music, more than any other attribute, is the defining characteristic of contemporary worship. To understand this, imagine worship in a service with a relaxed liturgy, comfortably dressed people, folks drinking coffee in the sanctuary — seems contemporary, right? Now imagine in that same setting all of the songs were traditional hymns led by a choir and a pipe organ. For most of us, the music would turn that contemporary setting into a traditional worship experience.

Now imagine this scene the other way around. Perhaps there is a formal sanctuary with men wearing ties, the women wearing dresses, and a reverent, high-church liturgy. This setting feels very traditional, but if all the songs are led by a band, complete with drums and electric guitars, the worship service would become inescapably contemporary. Clearly, music is the determining factor that defines whether worship is traditional or contemporary in these examples. For this reason and for the fact that music makes up at least half of the content of our worship services in most denominational churches, music will be a primary concern in this book.

2. Music is Important in Worship

> "If music be the food of love, play on."
>   —William Shakespeare[3]

Try this experiment: Imagine you are in a beautiful open field surrounded by flowers, trees, sunshine and breeze. If you close your eyes, what are the sounds you hear? Do you hear birds singing? Do you hear the quiet hum of bees landing on flowers? Do you hear the breeze flowing through the nearby trees? Do you hear the crickets?

Imagine all of those sounds going silent. As we imagine this silence, a feeling of emptiness is generated. Something is missing, something vital to the experience.

Now, imagine those sounds coming back in. The birds are singing again, the bees are humming, the crickets are chirping, the breeze is gently stirring the trees. With these sounds, everything is right again, everything in God's creation is back in order. This is the music of creation. These sounds help us to imagine what that open field looks like, smells like, how the breeze feels. These sounds open up our senses to a fuller experience of creation. This is what music does in worship. Music can sharpen our imaginations as we gather collectively to wonder about God. Music, perhaps even more than spoken words, can tell a story that evokes memories, awakens mental images and stirs our emotions.

Probably the best way to understand the importance of music in worship is to imagine a service with absolutely no music: no instruments, no singing, no chanting, no hymns, nothing. As we imagine worship without music, it seems too passive and too one-dimensional for telling God's story. Now imagine a worship service filled with music. Imagine instruments, liturgies being sung, grown-ups and children singing, percussion, and pipe organs. Now that's more like it!

In his book *Music and Theology*, Don E. Saliers asserts that when we go to worship, we are not there just for information but for an experience. He writes: "Music has the power to engage more than the senses. It evokes our deeper nature, our truest selves, which is of God…we have an opportunity with music to sing and play with our whole being, making music is the language of the soul."[4] We experience music in ways that are not limited to our senses. Music can be like prayer, or it can be prayer itself in that it facilitates a connection with God.

Great thinkers throughout the centuries have remarked on the power and importance of music in worship. St Augustine wrote: "The tears flowed from me when I heard your hymns and canticles, for the sweet singing of your church moved me deeply. The music surged in my ears, truth seeped into my heart, and my feelings of devotion overflowed…"[5]

Martin Luther praised music as a wonderful gift from God. He wrote that next to the word of God, music deserves the highest praise. Martin Luther went on to say "after all, the gift of language combined with the gift of song was only given to man to let him know that he should praise God with both word and music, namely, by proclaiming the word of God through music."[6]

Music grounds us in our heritage and tells our stories. For example, the song "I'll be Home for Christmas" connects us to the anxious longing felt by American soldiers and their loved ones during World War II. African American spirituals connect us to the plight of persons living in slavery. Irish folk songs give us glimpses of joy and sorrow in Irish history. The song "Brother, Can You Spare a Dime?" expresses the struggle of the Great Depression. The song "We Shall Overcome" depicts the hopeful angst of the Civil Rights Movement. The Psalms themselves are songs that reflect the struggle and celebration of God's people in the ancient world. Because music tells our stories and connects us to our past, music is our legacy and our inheritance.

In his book *Theology, Music and Time*, Dr. Jeremy Begbie claims that music is a "living practice," it engages the physical world, it is "inescapably bodily, and it has very strong connections with our emotional life."[7] Music has the ability to make us feel. Contemporary music, which typically draws from a broader spectrum of musical styles and instrumentation, has a vast potential for creating experiences that evoke our emotions. Music in the form of songs or background music can guide our worship environment toward a particular state and assist in adding meaning to our liturgies. Music can excite us, it can compel us to be contemplative, it can inspire us to move our bodies and calm us to stillness. Music in worship can function like a sound track. Sound tracks to movies, for example, change the experience of movie going. Music has a similar potential for affecting the overall experience of worship.

When a song is offered to God, it becomes a prayer. We've all heard the phrase "She who sings, prays twice." There's wisdom in that statement. We know that music has a way of seeping into the crevices of our minds, affecting us in powerful ways. Music, unlike words alone, can evoke our emotions. When a song is delivered with passion, that passion becomes part of the message of that song. Music brings words to life. In worship, music helps us to find life in God's word.

3. Music Lasts

In 2008, my father passed away from Alzheimer's. This disease is called the "long goodbye" because of how it diminishes brain function gradually, stealing our ability to remember things. My father would eventually forget who he was and where he was, but he could remember old melodies. At times he would forget his grandchildren's names, but he never forgot the lyrics to "Earth Angel." Music is stored in our long-term memory and can become a grounding force and a spiritual plateau as we age. We carry music with us, even when our faculties fail. Familiar refrains come back to us from the recesses of our brains.

Worship leaders take note: the songs we prepare and lead stick with people in profound ways. Even if the message of the song doesn't sink in, the melodies are stored in our brains. Sermons can't do that, at least not in the same way or to the same extent. Through our songs, we can help create the building blocks of faith for young people while their long-term memories are forming. These songs can be a lifeline for older folks whose memories are becoming less reliable.

Church music matters. It's good and right to take seriously what we do as worship leaders, considering that our music can outlive us.

4. Music: A Tool to Discover Theology

Those of us who lead contemporary worship accept that theology is embedded in music we make. Music can be used to enhance our understanding of the divine. It engages time and space, and it is both bodily and external. For this, music is useful for Process, Systematic and Comparative Theology.

Dietrich Bonhoeffer used musical language for much of his theology. He found healing and hope, even while in prison, in the interrelatedness between music and the divine.[8] Karl Barth and Hans Küng both appreciate the theological value of Mozart and consider Bach a theologian who communicates his theology through movement to music.[9]

Hildegard of Bingen, a theologian, composer and Benedictine Abbess, considers music as a fundamental resource for theological instruction. She argues that music played a crucial role in reforming the church, specifically in the administration of the sacraments. She likens musical harmony with the right relationship with God, which is restored and maintained through confession and communion.[10]

Jeremy Begbie considers music to be a divine gift that can give us insight to the nature of God. He uses music, specifically improvisational jazz, as a direct metaphor for understanding the mysterious work of the Holy Spirit.[11]

Section 2

Contemporary Worship: Are We There Yet?

Finding Balance in the Tension Moving Forward

1. General History

2. Sacred Music

3. Transcendence versus Immanence

1. General History

A few years ago, I interviewed my former professor Dr. Bill Leonard, Founding Dean of the Wake Forest University School of Divinity and Dunn Professor of Baptist Studies and Church History. I asked him to talk about the origins of contemporary worship as defined by its relative juxtaposition to traditional worship. He said that the origins of American contemporary worship, which is a reflection of its surrounding culture, can be found in the beginnings of American Protestantism. He pointed out that the Puritans had broken ties from their European traditions, forming the Congregational Tradition in the 16th Century. Worship for these early Puritans was simple as compared to their English religious heritage, and it was reflective of their present congregational identity. Consequently, worship in the Congregational Tradition was a degree less formal than the religious practices they moved away from.

When we think of contemporary worship, we don't think of the Puritans. But when we consider that their worship was radically different from their heritage and was shaped by their current reality or context, it is fair to define their worship style as contemporary.[12]

Bill Leonard went on to say the most tangible origins to what we consider contemporary worship in the United States can be found in the frontier movement, specifically the Great Awakenings.[13] As Christians moved westward in the United States, worship began incorporating elements of frontier culture, not necessarily jettisoning traditional worship but adapting worship to fit a new, multi-cultural environment. Leonard argues the frontier movement presented similar challenges we face today in reaching the "nones" or persons without a formal religious identity. Early American frontier Christians had to offer worship that immediately engaged new people, regardless of their specific religious heritage or lack thereof.

Some religious traditions in the New World chose not to adapt, at least initially, to the New World culture. Instead they chose to preserve their Old World religious heritage. Early American Lutherans, for example, vigorously held to traditional worship that was consistent with their European origins. In so doing, these New World Lutherans galvanized their American congregations to the relative exclusion of non-Lutherans. Early German immigrants found comfort in worship that was forged in their heritage, and they became a tight-knit social group. For them, evangelistic enterprise was more focused on assimilating others to their way of worship verses adapting the worship they offered to the cultural context in which they found themselves. It was more important to them to preserve their religious heritage than to accommodate a new population. The Lutheran church eventually changed its posture to be more inviting and adaptive to people who are not lifelong Lutherans, but a similar tension between preservation and evangelism still exists in the ELCA, if not all major denominations.

This tension between preserving tradition and adapting for growth guided the conversation as to how to do worship in the early American church and continues to guide our conversations today. Within this tension, Christians weigh choices about worship in terms of sacred and secular.

2. Sacred Music

Bill Leonard considers the debate over sacred versus secular is a significant thread in the development of contemporary Christian worship. In denominational churches throughout the United States, this debate is still hotly contested and continues to shape our approaches to worship. Music, more than anything else, defines contemporary worship and the debate over whether contemporary worship music is sacred enough or too secular. This issue remains a source of friction as we move forward.

This debate is much older than North American Christianity. Music in general has been exalted and scrutinized throughout Christian history. We perpetually try to define sacred music, a phrase that remains a moving target throughout church history. In every historical period, contemporary music finds its way into churches and synagogues, always with tension, resulting in paradigmatic shifts to our understanding of sacredness.

The earliest Christian churches struggled with the use of music. Don Saliers cites that music in general in the first century was suspect because of its close associations with theatre, Roman bourgeois and with pagan religions. The early Christian church found certain forms of music problematic, especially instrumental music with dancing, which was associated with the immoral practices of Roman and Greek cultures. The early Christian church considered the theatre and its music to be a form of idolatry and considered ecstatic dancing to be profane. They rejected instrumental music because of how its meaning was co-opted by sinful behavior. For example, playing the lyre was associated with prostitution. At that time and place, the idea of playing the lyre in worship would have been considered anathema.

As the New Testament church evolved into the early Christian church with its ever widening scope of appeal, they encountered a more diverse and influential set of musical forces within their multicultural context. Eventually, these forces would break through early Christians' resolutions to ban music from worship. We see this in the practice of chanting for worship, a practice heavily influenced by Roman and Galatian culture.[14]

The practice of chanting in western Christian churches was endorsed and perpetuated by St. Ambrose, Bishop of Milan, who was also a composer. Ambrose relied on and demonstrated the power of music when his basilica was under siege in 386 CE as part of the Arian Conflict. In response, those faithful to Ambrose occupied the basilica, and in their fearful angst they were sustained by the songs they sang. St. Augustine was deeply moved by this event. He wrote:

> "It was then that the practice was established of singing hymns and Psalms in the manner customary in regions in the East, to prevent people losing heart and fainting from weariness."[15]

In his *Confessions*, Augustine lauds the effect the music created in the Milanese Basilica had on him. He writes:

"How copiously I wept at your hymns and canticles...Those voices flooded my ears, and the truth was distilled in my heart until it overflowed in loving devotion; my tears ran down, and I was better for them."[16]

Saint Augustine fully supported music in worship, but he was worried that its impact on our emotions could stir up lustful responses, leading us to sin. He was concerned with structuring a way to harness the positive benefits of music while restricting music's potential to ignite passions in people, driving them toward desires of the flesh. Essentially, Augustine wanted to delineate music in terms of sacred and secular. Toward this end, he wrote his lesser known treatise titled "On Music." Don H. Compier summarizes this work by claiming it is primarily concerned with establishing what kind of music will have the right ethical effects. From "On Music," Compier notes that Augustine, who was heavily influenced by platonic philosophy, concludes:

"Good music allows us to rationally perceive the divinely ordered pattern in nature, which we must follow in order to have a life pleasing to God. Bad music influences our immaterial soul through our senses material senses, and should be avoided."[17]

Augustine insists that reason is needed to harness the positive effects of music and govern the risk of sin stirred through an emotional response to music. For Augustine, music has to make intellectual sense. This explains in part his concern and prohibition over non-verbal music.

Augustine does not support completely banning music from worship, but he wanted to safeguard believers against the seductive power of music. He cited the use of frenzied musical worship among pagans as well as his rivals, the Donatists.[18] Augustine considered the Donatists to be heretical and their worship to be invalid, if not sinful. He argued that without the regulation of rational thought, music runs amok with impulsive sensual fervor working to corrupt our souls. If we were to

try to adapt Augustine's mandates on music in a modern setting, we would need to minimize instrumentation, harmony,
background vocals and anything that would distract from the
direct scriptural truths represented in our songs.

As music in general became more elaborate in the Medi-
eval and early Renaissance periods, we find worship music reflecting this evolution. Don Saliers cites how music in general
was scrutinized by the church in those eras. He notes that the
traditions of sacred music show constant attempts to separate
itself from secular society, while still borrowing musical devel-
opments from the larger culture. He writes, "this borrowing
was always modified by the religious tradition."[19]

Three and four-part polyphony would eventually become
the norm for sacred music in monasteries and cathedrals
throughout Europe. But this form of music, which was bor-
rowed from its surrounding culture, was once considered profane. For example, in 1180 John of Salisbury wrote:

> "(Polyphonic) music sullies the divine service...the sing-
> ers attempt, with the lewdness of a lascivious singing voice
> and a singularly foppish manner, to feminize all their spell-
> bound little followers with the girlish way they rendered the
> notes and end the phrases."[20]

Jean Calvin would share some of John of Salisbury's concerns, but he saw music as a useful tool for animating the
Psalms. Calvin recognized the importance of music as a vehicle for communion with God. Like Augustine, Calvin (who
was also influenced by Plato) sees music as a means by which
the heart can be positively affected through the guidance of
rational thought. In Calvin's *Institutes of the Christian Religion*,
he writes:

> "And surely, if the singing be tempered to that gravity
> which is fitting in the sight of God and the angels, it both lends
> dignity and grace to sacred actions and has the greatest value
> in kindling our hearts to a true zeal and eagerness to pray."[21]

Calvin distinguishes his thinking from Augustine by looking at music as a means through which the mind can be affected by an energized heart. He writes: "we do not condemn
speaking and singing provided they are associated with the
heart's affection and serve it for the state they do exercise the
mind in thinking of God and keep it attentive."[22]

Calvin also departs from Augustine in the way he confronts
his rival, the Catholic Church. Where Augustine condemns the
ecstatic use of music by the Donatists, Calvin criticizes the Roman Catholic church for offering music that is too cold and
distant and for avoiding music altogether. Calvin writes:

> "The Psalms can incite us to lift up our hearts to God... the
> Pope and those that belong to him have deprived the Church;
> for he has reduced the Psalms, which ought to be true spiritual
> songs, to a murmuring among themselves without any under-
> standing."[23]

Calvin, like Augustine, insists that music makes sense in-
tellectually. Moreover, he finds value in music's ability to stir
us to appropriate levels of passion and awe for God. Calvin
was very concerned about human depravity stealing or distort-
ing the effectiveness of music in worship. He was adamantly
against the use of hymns and insisted that only the Psalms be
sung. He concluded that the Psalms are holy in their essence,
divine in their creation and communication through Scripture.
Calvin was critical of the human contribution to hymns that
reflect Scripture but are not directly scriptural.

Martin Luther would disagree with Calvin on the use of
hymns. Luther, himself a composer and musician, was also
heavily influenced by Augustine. Luther found respite in music throughout his tumultuous life, developing a deep affection and appreciation for the theological, liturgical and personally spiritual value of music.[24] Luther breaks slightly from his
Augustinian tradition as he writes about music. Luther cites
Augustine's concern over music's influence and potential to
lead to sin, but he sharply disagrees with his contemporaries

who would use Augustine's reservations as grounds for banning music in worship. Luther writes:

> "I have no use for cranks who despise music, because it is a gift from God. Music drives away the devil and makes people gay; they forget thereby all wrath, unchastity, arrogance, and the like. Next after theology I give music the highest place and the greatest honor."[25]

Where Augustine feared that music could lead people toward sin, Luther extols music's potential to protect us from sin. Martin Luther, affirming his belief in the priesthood of all believers, invited the congregation to be active contributors to the music offered in worship. He led choral practices with his congregants and encouraged them to practice at home. Using the new technology of the printing press, Luther compiled hymnals and distributed them among the community. Luther saw music as a unifying force and hoped it would help hold Christians together through the upheaval of reformation.

Martin Luther loved polyphony and encouraged instrumentation. Luther was much more liberal in his understanding than Augustine and Calvin as to what qualifies as sacred music. Luther applauded the use of hymns and encouraged an ever-widening songbook beyond the Psalms. He found theological value in harmony and instrumental music. Luther's thinking on music was not a complete departure from Augustine, however. Martin Luther also had some concerns over music being used toward sinful ends. Luther writes: "take care to shun perverted minds who prostitute this lovely gift of nature and of art with their erotic rantings."[26] Luther acknowledges that music, like money or sex, can be used for sinful intentions but is in essence a divine gift with profound divine purpose and completely appropriate for worship.

Luther's somewhat distant fellow reformer Ulrich Zwingli would disagree on the liturgical worth of music. Zwingli, an instrumental reformer from Switzerland as well as an accomplished musician, insisted that organs and singing be excluded from worship. He knew how emotionally powerful music was, and he did not want it to be a sensual distraction from the pure word of God. The church in his view should be separate from the entertainments of society and free from distraction. With some irony, Zwingli did insist that musical instruction be part of the core curriculum in schools, accrediting musical training as part of a balanced education. Even more ironic is how Zwingli wrote songs as resources for when Christians are "attacked by pestilence."[27] Zwingli valued worship as sacred and music as secular and was deliberate about keeping them separate.

John Wesley and his brother Charles Wesley would establish their own tact on the subject of sacred music. Disagreeing with Zwingli, John Wesley was very much moved and sustained by music and thought it appropriate for worship. John Wesley also disagreed with Calvin in declaring that worship music can and should go beyond the Psalms. Mostly composed by Charles and then compiled and instituted by John, the Wesley brothers created new hymnals written to reflect scriptural themes in an expressive, common vernacular. Charles Wesley allowed secular culture to heavily influence his writing, borrowing melodies from English and German folk songs, choral tunes, opera and theater music.

John Wesley shared the concerns of Augustine, Calvin, Luther and Zwingli as to the seductive nature of music. Wesley was more concerned, however, with this affect stemming from popular music in general, not church music. He differs from Martin Luther in his thoughts on how music is offered. In his writing "Thoughts on the power of music," Wesley condemns modern music for its use of harmony, which he calls "counterpoint." He argues that the use of harmony distorts the power and functionality of music as a resource for worship. Wesley concluded that the modern popular music of his time failed to stir people emotionally and convey meaning and, for this reason, it should be avoided. John and Charles Wesley sharply disagreed on this point, however.[28]

Supporters of contemporary worship love to talk about how Martin Luther and Charles Wesley used melodies from popular songs sung in local pubs in the compositions they used in worship. The extent to which this actually happened is hotly debated. I tried to get Dean Leonard, professor of Church History at Wake Forest University, to weigh in on this topic, but he wouldn't commit since there is strong evidence on both sides of the debate. Instead, he pointed out the fact that many of us want this to be true, and the fact that many of us don't is a revealing look at the current landscape of Christianity as it relates to contemporary worship.[29]

Since it's unclear whether this happened or not, we are left to form opinions based on what we know about Luther and Wesley within their historical context. Personally, I like to think about Martin Luther, a musician himself, playing stringed instruments in worship, borrowing pub melodies for songs like "A Mighty Fortress is Our God." I also like what Adam Hamilton, a renown Wesley scholar, has to say on the subject. He writes:

> "...all of Charles Wesley's songs were contemporary when they were written. Charles Wesley, along with a handful of others, played a key role in introducing hymns that put into every day words and phrases the themes of the faith and experiences believers had of God's Grace."[30]

If we fast forward to the early 20th Century, we see the debate over what music is to be considered sacred took a formal turn in 1903 when Pope St. Pius X issued his *Motu Propio* on Sacred Music. Within this declaration, the Pontiff shows favor to vocal music, especially chanting, while strictly forbidding most instrumentation beyond the organ, unless there are qualifying circumstances.[31] Here are some examples of the prohibitions from his edict:

> 15. Although the music proper to the Church is purely vocal music, music with the accompaniment of the organ is also permitted. In some special cases, within due limits and with proper safeguards, other instruments may be allowed, but never without the special permission of the [bishop of the diocese], according to the requirements of the *Caeremoniale Episcoporum* [the Ceremonial for Bishops].[32]

19. The employment of the piano is forbidden in church, as is also that of noisy or frivolous instruments such as drums, cymbals, bells and the like.[33]

20. It is strictly forbidden to have bands play in church, and only in special cases with the consent of the Ordinary will it be permissible to admit wind instruments, limited in number, judiciously used, and proportioned to the size of the place provided the composition and accompaniment be written in grave and suitable style, and conform in all respects to that proper to the organ.[34]

It absolutely fascinates me to see how the Catholic Church has changed over the last century concerning its understanding of sacred music. Pianos are staples in most Catholic churches and more and more have bands playing music on Sundays and Saturday evenings, despite these being clear violations of what Pope Pius X declared to be sacred a century ago. Sacredness is clearly a moving target for the Catholic faith, as well as for all Christian denominations. Because church and culture are inescapably symbiotic, we should expect culture to continually change and push forward our musical expressions in worship.

Jeremy Begbie writes: "In musicology it has become commonplace to emphasize the social and cultural embeddedness of musical practices"[35] He suggests that in order to understand or study music, we have to know something about the culture that affects it. Begbie makes it clear that culture shapes and defines music by affecting its creation as well as the way it is received. He reminds us that music is an extension of our culture, it's part of who we are. From this, I would argue that the music we use in worship should also reflect who we are.

It is natural for church music to change as a reflection of culture. As music changes, our preferences may not. We should not conflate preference with sacredness. Instead, we should look to ascribe sacredness to the object of our worship, not the means by which we worship our God. With this, I would challenge all of us to widen our understanding of what qualifies as sacred music.

Renowned composer Sir John Tavener says that "the whole purpose of sacred music must lead us to the threshold of prayer or to the threshold of a true encounter with the living God."[36] It would make sense by his assessment that any form of music that accomplishes the task of leading us to prayerful encounters with God should be considered sacred.

Because our definitions of sacredness are so heavily influenced by our cultural contexts, it is imperative we create our definitions to be dynamic, to adapt to and hopefully transcend our culture so that they remain useful. Over the centuries, church dogma has proven to be insufficient in permanently defining our directives on music. Perhaps we should ask questions like, "Does this music move me closer to God or further away from God? Does this music inspire wonder? Does this music challenge us to seek justice, kindness and peace? Does it reflect the hope of the Gospels?" Perhaps music itself cannot be sacred, but the purposes for which it is offered can justify music as a means toward that sacred end.

3. Transcendence versus Immanence

Bill Leonard said that instead of thinking of worship today in terms of sacred verses secular, we should evaluate worship in terms of "transcendence and immanence." Transcendence in this case refers to God being mystical, beyond us, and yet to come. Immanence, in this case, refers to God being with us, the Kingdom of God being here and now. Dean Leonard claims that the emergent church has formed in part to offer an alternative to traditional denominational forms of worship that are too focused on transcendence (high church — God is far away in heaven) and contemporary, often nondenominational forms of worship that are too focused on the immanent (folksy — God is with us).

As we endeavor to offer meaningful worship, albeit contemporary or traditional, we do well to offer music, rituals and other worship actions that celebrate God's transcendence as well as God's immanence. Worship that captures the awe and mystery of God with appropriate reverence, while still being accessible and personal, is ideal.[37]

How we offer music in church can do much to convey this two-fold image of God. For example, if what we offer is a huge, professionally done, high art, unapproachable body of songs, it's possible the image of God we project is also high and unapproachable. If we offer songs that are too folksy, cute and pedestrian, we risk showing improper reverence. Where sacred and secular function as exclusive, binary statements, transcendence and immanence operate more on a scale or spectrum. As we forge our images and understandings of contemporary worship and how it will function, weighing our choices against transcendence verses immanence allows us more flexibility in being both contemporary and traditional at the same time.

Section 3

Sticking with Traditional

1. What's Wrong with Tradition?

2. "Hospitable Traditionalism"

3. What We Mean by Relevant

4. Growing Traditional Worship

1. What's Wrong with Tradition?

Kelly Fryer, an ELCA pastor, author and professor, writes "there is nothing wrong with tradition unless tradition has become your God."[38] Fryer warns us to keep our focus on God and avoid placing our devotion on the man-made practices we developed in response to God. As we allow our understanding of sacredness to live, breathe and evolve, it is imperative that we continually weigh our traditions against the Gospel. Here is an exercise that demonstrates what it looks like when we worship tradition:

Imagine you are in the middle of your church's worship service, with all sorts of voices singing and praising God. Now imagine someone coming in and interrupting your worship service demanding that everyone stop! And then they exclaim, "You all should repent for blaspheming God by having WOMEN sing in worship!"

In this scenario, most of us would deem this person out of order and ask them to discontinue their rant. We should recognize, however, that at times in ecclesiastical history it would be scandalous for women to sing in church. The "indignant ranter" in this exercise would be very much in order in centuries past and applauded for his resolve.

This exercise is an extreme example of what it looks like when we allow our traditions to be our gods. As time moves on and cultures change, we see Scripture with fresh perspectives. And although God's word does not change, the way we hear it, understand it, and apply it does. For the "indignant ranter" who interrupted the worship service in this example, his value systems were offended. The god he worships wants things a certain way, and his god sees women as lesser beings. To challenge his interpretation, his value system, is to challenge his god. His value system is his god.

We all risk worshiping tradition when we set our focus on the way we worship instead of the God we intend to worship. Tradition is valuable and important. It connects us to our past and builds a bridge to our future. In order for tradition to survive, however, it has to be flexible. Traditions are determined by the people who live within cultures. People and cultures change. Tradition is most valuable when it meets us where we are, when it connects us, invites us, and represents not only the God who inspired the tradition but the generations who gave us this gift.

When tradition is used to exclude people, however, we run the risk of bearing the same rebukes that Jesus volleyed at the Pharisees and Scribes. Jesus was serious when he challenged the religiously self-righteous of his day. He meant it when he called them out for using religious tradition to exclude people, other children of God. So how do we address this? How do we uphold tradition without letting it become our God, without using it to make others outside of our traditions feel lesser-than or excluded? Bill Leonard offers some advice for living in this balance. He calls this approach "Hospitable Traditionalism."

2. Hospitable Traditionalism

Bill Leonard offers an alternative for denominational churches who want to reach out to their communities without necessarily adding contemporary worship. He suggests that congregations adopt a strategy he calls "Hospitable Traditionalism."[39] He writes:

> "Congregations need to begin by reaffirming their spiritual identity, a sense of who they are under God. . . . a people bound together by powerful ideas, rituals, and histories amid a continuing quest for faith, grace and perhaps even justice. This traditionalism is hospitable when it turns persons outward on the world, not inward on themselves."[40]

This strategy turns congregants into ambassadors representing our faith traditions within our communities. Hospitable traditionalism sets the table for inviting persons who are not raised in our traditions to be more easily assimilated into full engagement in our worship services and church community life. If we want to grow and incorporate more people into our faith traditions, we will need to create an accessible environment that predicates inclusion on decisions of faith, not just a common history or birthright. The more we can develop a culture of inclusion, the more successful we will be in adding new people to our communities.

Here's a metaphor that may be helpful: I like protein shakes. The whey protein I drink is really good for me, although it doesn't dissolve well in milk. It clumps up, and the milk is still milk while the protein is wet glops of goo. When I warm the milk, however, it blends nicely. If new people are like protein powder and our worship is like milk, we need to find ways to "warm up" our worship so that we can be more effectively integrated.

Bill Leonard suggests that we can warm up our congregations by actively using traditions to engage new members. He recommends using "Guide to Worship" pamphlets that explain our liturgical traditions and guide visitors through worship, so they feel less lost and out of place.[41] Leonard reminds us that the "method affects the message"[42] and invites congregations to consider ways to use tradition to be invitational and inclusive.

Now go back to the scenario from the previous section. Imagine the indignant intruder disrupting our worship service. What do we do with this person? Do we ask him or her to leave? Do we ignore this person? Is the liturgy this person disrupted more important than the person? Tough questions.

If we strive to be hospitable within our traditions, we will need to work to include all people, even those who are challenging and disagreeable. So now let us draw out some possible endings for our scenario: First, imagine that the congregation confronts the interrupter and forbids this person to return. This probably doesn't feel very "Jesus-y."

Next, imagine that we give in and adjust to the demands of the person who interrupts. That feels cowardly. Finally, imagine some care-giving congregants who take this person aside while worship continues. These caregivers invite the interrupter to listen to the diverse voices singing in harmony and challenge this person to listen for God through these voices until worship concludes.

Perhaps these caregivers will assure the interrupter that his concerns will be discussed and considered after worship. In this last (best case) scenario, the congregation respects its traditions as well as the people who challenge them.

3. What We Mean by Relevant

A buzzword in contemporary worship is the word relevant. There's even a magazine called *Relevant* that highlights cutting-edge spiritual music. Personally I like to use the word because it helps define a good characteristic we want to see in all forms of worship. By saying that our worship is relevant, we're saying we are offering worship in a way that meets people where they are and has meaning to them.

There is, however, a dangerous and pervasive notion that the term relevant is exclusive to contemporary worship. A quick perusal of the blogosphere surrounding contemporary worship illustrates how several Christians assert that contemporary worship, as opposed to traditional worship, does a better job of meeting people where they are. This is patently untrue.

Contemporary music and contemporary worship does a good job of finding new paths and reaching new people and helps broaden the overall relevance of religion in general. Contemporary worship is not, however, superior to traditional worship in providing meaningful worship experiences to believers.

If relevance is our goal, we should look at it as a comprehensive strategy. Contemporary worship is going to be more relevant to some worshipers. Traditional worship is going to be more relevant to others.

When we say that one particular style is relevant, we could be indirectly making a claim the other worship styles are not relevant. As we use the word relevant, it helps to remember that relevance itself is relevant to its context.

4. Growing Traditional Worship

Often denominational churches assume the only way to grow and to reach new members is to start a contemporary worship service. This is not true. Contemporary worship is an effective means of creating energy and accessibility to a broader demographic, but it's not the only way to grow. To increase engagement in traditional worship, there are several aspects that can be looked at, addressed, and enhanced.

Starting with music, a congregation that worships exclusively in a traditional mode should invest in training its children how to sing within a choir. Children's choirs, workshops, musical training within Sunday school, musical training within any church provided day care are all means of increasing participation in traditional worship music. Many people who gravitate toward contemporary worship find they just are unable to sing well to hymns. They can't read music and are unsure how to sing with other people. If they had training on how to sing from the hymnal, they would likely benefit more from traditional worship. This is not a quick fix, but a long-term strategy for maintaining participation and vibrancy in traditional worship.

Next, it's important to celebrate and remind congregations of the meanings of long-standing rituals. Traditional worship is defined by its liturgy and rituals. Taking time to discuss the meaning of liturgical events and rituals and targeting them toward meeting the needs of the congregation can powerfully enhance your congregation's experience in worship. It's important that the liturgy and rituals within worship not become motions we simply go through but rather are all celebrations with renewed meaning each week.

Also, consider ways to make traditional worship more inviting and accessible to potential newcomers. For example, one church I worked for learned there was a prevalent misconception held by parents of babies that they would not be welcome in the more formal traditional services. These parents operated under the assumption that if their babies cried, like babies do, it would disrupt the service, and they would be made to feel embarrassed. To address this misconception, we talked openly about it with parents with young children, asking them to let go of these fears. We placed a rocking chair with baby blankets in the worship space for any parent to use during worship. The rocking chair is a physical reminder to everyone that babies are welcome, and parents with little ones are encouraged to come and be part of worship.

Section 4

Ch- Ch- Ch- Changes
Turning to Face the Strange Shifts in Our Religious Culture

1. Religion and Culture

2. Choirs are Evolving

3. Plug and Play

4. Words Change

5. Lyrics Change

6. Flexibility in the Moment

1. Religion and Culture

Religion is inescapably bound with culture. Paul Tillich, a systematic theologian, devotes considerable thought to this notion. He explains that religion is formed from culture and vice versa. Tillich asserts that religion and culture share a common substance. He claims there is a symbiotic synergy between culture and religion. Tillich writes:

> "Such a relationship definitely prevents the establishment of a dualism between religion and culture. Every religious act, not only in organized religion but also in the most intimate movement of the soul, is culturally formed."[43]

Tillich cites that culture helps to create and define religion while religion helps to create and define culture. I find Tillich's theology helpful in looking at contemporary worship as a natural response to the interconnection between religion and culture. Many of us resist the influence of popular culture infiltrating our religious practices. Tillich reminds us this is natural, necessary and unavoidable. Likewise, it is natural, necessary and unavoidable that our religion influences our culture.

Live contemporary worship music is witnessed more in American culture than any other type of live music. When we consider the thousands of people in thousands of churches across our country listening to live contemporary worship music each week, it's easy to assume that no other form of live music even comes close to the number of people in attendance. I see this as an opportunity to convey the Gospel through music in a way that profoundly affects our culture.

In his book *Gods and Guitars: Seeking the Sacred in Post-1960s Popular Music*, Michael J. Gilmour writes about how religious themes have had and continue to have a huge impact on popular music.[44] He, like Paul Tillich, recognizes a symbiotic relationship between culture and religion. This is a good thing. This relationship allows us who love the Gospel to tell the story in ever-changing, dynamic ways in our churches, and it allows us to take the Gospel message outside our church walls by affecting our broader culture.

Here's an example of how this works: At a church I worked
for, we decided to play a song by Matisyahu called "One Day."
The song is written by a Hasidic Jew and has reggae and hip-
hop elements. It is a beautiful song with a really thick beat that
depicts a dream of a better, more peaceful world. The song was
very popular among teenagers at the time. It was a commercial
success but not considered Christian music. When we played
it, some of our youth became immediately more engaged and
were excited about the song. For many of our retired congregants, this was their first time hearing it. And they loved it,
too! One 79-year-old woman went home and was still singing
the song later in the day. Her grandson, who wasn't at church
that day, heard her and started singing along with her, creating a wonderful and unique connection. Religion and culture
influenced each other with a joyful reciprocity that day, connecting generations through a meaningful experience.

Guy Beck in his book *Sacred Sound – Experiencing Music and
World Religions* explores how the center of gravity in Christianity is shifting from the North Atlantic world of Europe and
North America to the Southern Hemisphere.[45] In order to function as globally aware and welcoming members of the Christian faith, we should be proactive in incorporating cultural influence from our increasingly-less-foreign Christian family in
Africa and Central and South America.

Contemporary worship music provides a terrific avenue
for this initiative. With a more diverse portfolio of instrumentation, contemporary worship music can add instruments from
different cultures more easily. Contemporary music, which is
way more likely to use drums than traditional music, is a closer relative to the more rhythmic sounds from African and Latin
churches.

Guy Beck on a different yet related topic asserts there are
"fundamental shifts concerning the place of music in popular culture. Musical training, for centuries the yardstick a
good education, increasingly has only a limited place in many
schools."[46] I would add that contemporary worship can function as an effective response to this cultural shift. Where traditional worship music requires considerably more musical

training to participate, contemporary worship allows people with limited musical training to sing, clap or play along.

2. Choirs are Evolving

Let's be honest! We are not learning how to sing in choirs like we used to. Most churches have children's choirs, but as I explore churches around the country, it's becoming more difficult to find kids older than 12 singing in any kind of choir. What this means is that we are not teaching our youth how to sing in parts or read music. Most children's choirs have all the children sing just the melody. So unless the skills are picked up somewhere else later in life, they will not be able to sing harmony, read notes, or be familiar with commonly used choral pieces. Without any training, it is difficult for congregants to fully sing along in or with the choir. People are less engaged when hymns are sung as a result.

A few people with whom I spoke said they are "counting verses," waiting for hymns to be over in traditional worship. I have to imagine that with some training, these folks could become exponentially more engaged in traditional music, especially if they feel as if they were contributing to the quality of the congregational music by lending their voices. As worship leaders, we can address the issue of declining participation in traditional worship by offering programs that teach young people how to sing in and along with choirs.

3. Plug and Play

The phrase "plug-and-play" comes from the world of personal computing. It means a device or peripheral can be plugged into the computer and start functioning immediately without having to install drivers or other complicated measures. I would contend that contemporary worship has been successful in reaching new members for churches primarily because it has a similar plug-and-play orientation.

For many of us, denominational worship is something you are born into. I grew up Roman Catholic, and there was a lot I needed to learn before I could fully participate in worship. Most Protestant denominations are similar. Traditional worship for Lutherans, Episcopalians, Methodists, Presbyterians and Baptists, for example, all require you have some training in order to be a fully functioning worshiper within that denomination. The idea of plug-and-play suggests that someone could come in without any training or preparation and fully engage in worship.

Contemporary worship often uses a more relaxed liturgy that does not require considerable training in order to stay on the same page as the other members of the congregation. Contemporary songs do not require you have specific training on how to read notes or sing along with a choir. In fact, the notes are rarely provided for songs. Congregations in contemporary worship usually have song lyrics projected for them instead of using hymnals. Because these words are higher than eye level, our heads must be up in order to read them. This gets our noses out of our hymnals and invites the congregation to a posture that is more inclusive, alert, and engaged. This posture is ideal for singing as well.

When liturgical events in contemporary worship are clearly defined and clearly instructed, someone who has never worshiped with you before will know what to do and feel less like an outsider. Paying attention to creatively explaining the sacraments and elements, coupled with clear instructions as to how to participate, will do well in creating the plug-and-play environment we are seeking.

A commitment to a plug-and-play strategy should guide everything from song selection, choices on vocal leadership, multimedia, investments in technology, marketing, and even the sermons. This does not mean, however, that we should choose a cafeteria-style approach. None of us can create worship that will be everything to everyone. There may be some elements in our worship we may want to leave as acquired tastes. I would certainly never suggest "dumbing down" our strategies on song selection and liturgy in order to increase mass appeal.

I will say that in order to be plug-and-play, we first need to claim our identity. We should figure out who it is we are and what's important to us in worship. Then figure out ways to make that work for everybody, including people who did not grow up within our traditions. I found that people who do not grow up within a particular tradition tend to appreciate many of the liturgical elements some lifelong members of a faith tradition might take for granted. For example, I recently had a conversation with someone who was new to Catholicism, and he explained how much he appreciated the stations of the cross. Having grown up Catholic, I was aware of the stations of the cross and at times walked prayerfully through them. But his appreciation for this symbol was a revelation to me as to their symbolic value.

Much like immigrants who have a heightened awareness of the freedoms we find in the United States, people who are new to our traditions remind us of how viable they are. In a way, plug-and-play strategies work to invite religious immigrants to share in our fellowship and bring renewed vigor for us to the traditions that have carried us this far.

4. Words Change

Etymology is the study of words. This discipline works to explain the origins of words and the meaning assigned to them. What a word means or symbolizes can change over time since we ascribe meaning to words based on their context. Because this context is shaped by culture and culture changes, words must also change. This is a particular issue in Biblical scholarship as we attempt to take words that meant something different in the ancient world and use them to apply meaning in today's cultural context. This challenge has resulted in vast differences in interpretation and is the reason why we have so many different translations of the Bible.

For example, let's compare a verse from the King James Version with the New Revised Standard Version. The King James Version of Isaiah 1:17 says: "Learn to do well; seek judgment, relieve the oppressed, judge the fatherless, plead for the widow." Now look at the New Revised Standard Version of the same text: "Learn to do good; seek justice, rescue the oppressed, defend the orphan, plead for the widow." We can see this is the same Scripture saying the same things, but the King

James Version is reflective of a different time. The King James Version, originally translated centuries earlier than the NRSV, equates the act of judging with the act of defending.

In today's vernacular, judging and defending are vastly different verbs. Also, the word "fatherless" in the ancient world was synonymous with the word orphan. Today, the two words are quite different in their meaning. This is an important distinction in that there are many homes in today's culture where fathers are not present. Single moms are playing both roles and, as hard as it is growing up without a dad, we wouldn't want to call someone in that situation an orphan. In the ancient world, however, being fatherless was synonymous to being an orphan. These are examples of how God's word does not change, but the culture we create does. The NRSV, as well as most other modern translations, uses words that better convey the meaning of the original text in today's language.

As a contemporary worship leader, I have had to update some of the words in the songs I prepared so that they were relevant in a modern context. I would encourage you to not make the mistake of considering songs that have been written a long time ago to be completely unchangeable. As we see with updated translations of Scripture, the words we use in translating Scripture change over time in order to maintain the original meaning within it. The words in our worship songs are no more sacred than the Scripture they are intended to represent.

5. Lyrics Change

God's word doesn't change, but the theology we create in response to God's word continues to change over the centuries. There may be some outdated theologies represented in some of our hymns; consequently, also in our hymnbooks. If you want to make a change to a classic hymn, in contemporary worship usually all you need to do is change it on the projection screen. In traditional worship, however, it's unrealistic to go to every hymnal and cross out and write in the words you want.

Here's an example: At my church, we decided we wanted much more emphasis on the life of Jesus instead of the death of Jesus when it comes to our salvation. Our church struggled with atonement language, as most denominational churches do. We decided we believe that the love of Jesus does as much to save us as the blood of Jesus. Since the words blood and love rhyme with each other, it was a common practice for us to switch those two words in some of our worship songs. With that simple switch, we made a powerful statement about how we believe Jesus actually saves us.

Atonement language is hotly debated throughout denominational worship, and I certainly don't want to try to change anyone's theology through this book. I just want to highlight how a simple change can make a powerful statement about your church's closely held beliefs. Also, several denominations are trying to use more inclusive language, which means replacing gender specific pronouns with non-gender specific ones. Whatever lyrical changes your church deems necessary for your songs, contemporary worship offers more immediate flexibility since you are not bound to a physical book.

6. Flexibility in the Moment

Contemporary worship offers flexibility on macro and micro levels. It allows us to respond to national worship trends, and it offers flexibility enough to respond to unexpected moments in congregational life. It is possible with contemporary worship to change the music and even the liturgy to help facilitate the celebration and mourning of current events.

Here are some examples: When a devastating tsunami hit Japan in 2011, my band led the congregation with a song called "40" by U2, which is taken directly from Psalm 40. During the last refrain, we sang in Japanese. When tragedy hit Sandy Hook Elementary, we changed our gathering song to "Soon and Very Soon." For this, we stepped out in front of the microphones and sang an a cappella version of the song, inviting the entire congregation to hold hands with us and sing as we collectively mourned this tragedy. Since we were projecting the lyrics, we were able to make these changes the morning of worship.

When the Boston Marathon was attacked in 2012, that Sunday we did a stripped-down version of the song "One Day" by Matisyahu, a song that is a vision for a world without such misguided, senseless violence. Because in worship we sing collectively, we have an opportunity to mourn, celebrate, doubt, hurt, find comfort, solidarity, renew our faith and heal together.

Contemporary worship can be flexible to accommodate celebrations as well. When we have special celebrations or events, we can take familiar songs that would normally not be heard in church and rewrite the words to fit the event. At one church I worked for, we rewrote the words for "Our House" by the band Madness in order to kick off a stewardship campaign at our church. The flexibility of contemporary worship, combined with the seemingly limitless catalog of music to pull from, provides worship leaders the opportunity to adapt on the fly to our ever-changing congregational life.

Pastors frequently ask congregations to challenge well-grooved ways of thinking. Often meditation on Scripture leads pastors to new understandings and interpretations that challenge the way they thought of them before. As musicians, we should also challenge ourselves to take on new ways of expressing music. We should endeavor to deepen our abilities and break free from well-rutted modes.

The Bible uses water as a symbol for life. Water that is not moving and changing is dead, stagnant. Living water flows, moves, brings life, carves out canyons and fills oceans. Our worship life must stay in motion. The church, like water, must respond to the world and be affected by it, knowing that over time it will shape it.

Section 5

Getting Started

1. Necessary Questions

2. Denominational Challenges

3. Visit Other Churches

1. Necessary Questions

A few years back, I sat down with Jeremy Begbie, a professor at Duke Divinity and arguably the world's foremost scholar on the topic of Theology and Music. I asked him to talk about contemporary worship and what advice he would give to a planning committee who was considering adding contemporary worship or revitalizing traditional worship. He suggested that any such effort begin with the question: "Who are these people (your target congregation) and how can we help these people experience God?"[47] This simple, yet profound question can guide our entire conversation about how to proceed with establishing worship in our churches. As we ask "Who are these people," we are drawn into an exercise of self-exploration, challenging us to identify who we are and who we want to be.

My suggestion to a committee would be to ask this question and try to answer it with single words, writing down the words your committee agrees best describe your ideal congregation. You may have words come up like: "families," "seekers," "stewards," "servants," "citizens." Then for each one of those words, ask the question, "How can we help _____ experience God?" For example, "How can we help families experience God?" "How can we help seekers experience God?" and so on. The answers to these questions will bring surprising clarity to your vision as you shape worship at your church.

After meeting with Jeremy Begbie, I met with Dr. Jill Crainshaw, a veteran pastor of Baptist and Presbyterian congregations and Blackburn Professor of Worship and Liturgical Theology at Wake Forest University School of Divinity. I asked her to give some advice from her particular expertise that would help congregations looking to start or improve contemporary worship at their church. She mentioned that we should consider what do we like in worship as a simple way of beginning. She said there are some important questions we should ask to continue the process.

The first question is "Why is worship important?" This is a great way to start our dreaming about what our worship could look like and in determining what we value as a congregation.

Dr. Crainshaw then suggests we ask the question, "Why do you come here?" In your committees, ask these questions and try to reduce the answers to single words or phrases. The list of words that result should be very descriptive and useful in defining your goals for worship. Crainshaw advises congregations to think about how their core values are represented in their worship models. As we make decisions about worship, she reminds us that the word liturgy literally means "the work of the people." This compels us to be as representative as we can of our whole congregation and our community at large.

Dr. Crainshaw draws a distinction between the words participatory and communal as they pertain to worship. If members of the congregation sit down and have a meal together, it would be communal. If members prepared a meal together, it would be participatory and communal. Increasing participation in executing worship may be a goal of your congregation. If so, think about ways the work of worship can be distributed and shared with several people instead of just clergy. To deepen a sense of community or to be more communal, consider ways to solidify your collective identity and sense of togetherness in worship. Create moments of affirmation during worship that reinforce your core values, building unity and shared moments in worship when we are invited to commune our hearts, minds, and spirits as well as our physical presence with each other.

Dr. Crainshaw agrees with Bill Leonard that effective worship strives for a balance between transcendence and immanence. She advises committees to ask the questions, "What does God look like?" and "Is God distant or close?" She submits that the answers to these questions can inform how we are doing and how we might achieve a balance between immanence and transcendence. She, like Bill Leonard, assesses that traditional worship most often favors the transcendence of God, where contemporary worship leans more toward God's immanence. Crainshaw suggests to committees charged with implementing contemporary worship to consider ways that you might build an awareness of God's transcendence in worship.

For example, sacraments like communion, confession and creeds connect us to centuries of Christian tradition and divine mysticism. Thoughtful inclusion of these elements in contemporary worship will build awe in a transcendent God while maintaining the more colloquial immanence associated with contemporary worship. Also, just about any worship event that focuses on life after death will increase our awareness of God's transcendence. Likewise, if you decide you want to build a focus on God's immanence, simple changes like preaching from the congregation's floor instead of the raised pulpit, allowing for applause after songs, congregational hand holding and liturgical foot washing all build community and increase our awareness of God among us.

Jill Crainshaw also advises congregations to avoid binaries when making choices about worship. Whether you are discussing traditional or contemporary, transcendent or immanent, individual or group, communal or participatory, she urges us to replace our "ors" with "ands" and not settle for black and white, but perhaps try to live in the grey. Finally, when developing worship, Jill asks us to consider the question, "What is home?" This is a profound question that leads us to celebrate what we love about our religious heritage and what we dream of creating when we build worship.[48]

2. Denominational Challenges

For those of us in denominational settings, contemporary music is defined by its juxtaposition to traditional music. Longtime traditional worshippers develop liturgical muscle memory. Those of us who grew up in traditional worship, through repetition and consistency, embrace it as part of our history, making it sacred to us. Offering worship that changes the way we've always done it can be considered a breath of fresh air by some and considered profane by others. Most denominations are centuries old, and we have to take care to make sure we proceed with respect, love, humility and openness.

There are liturgical elements that help define a denomination's worship identity. This means that in denominational worship, you're not starting with a blank slate. You have to find ways to satisfy the need for these elements so that the worship you provide retains your denominational identity. For example, if your denomination has communion, that should be part of your contemporary worship. It's relatively easy to adapt communion to a contemporary liturgy. If your denomination requires you say a creed at the beginning of each worship service or requires that a ordained pastor offers absolution following confession, these elements may be a little bit more difficult to accommodate, and they may be considered optional.

While in committee, decisions should be made as to what is necessary and what is optional. Let your pastors have considerable influence on making these choices. On these decisions, it could be helpful to seek input from your local synod, conference, diocese, presbyter, or other denominational governing body.

Throughout the history of Protestant worship, discussions over worship liturgies have unified as well as divided Christians. Be thoughtful and inclusive when you decide how you choose to honor or jettison these elements. Be respectful, but don't be afraid to question your denominational liturgy. There is a historical precedent for protestant denominations to question and attempt to continually reform their liturgy. Asking questions like, "Why is this sacred?" or "What purpose does this serve?" can guide your conversations.

My best advice is to form a representative committee taken from the entire congregation to discuss and weigh in on any changes you would like to make concerning liturgies. Make an effort to include traditional worshipers in your discussions on contemporary worship. They can give your committees valuable insight as you work to create a plug-and-play liturgy that is true to your denominational heritage.

3. Visit Other Churches

The benefit of visiting other churches and examining the way they approach contemporary worship is twofold. First, if there are things they do that you like, you can use their example to guide your work. Observing practices you may want to emulate at your church can challenge, motivate and inspire you. Second, if there are things you don't care for, you can use that to guide your work in avoidance of that practice. Also, it will help you celebrate what you're doing well at your church.

Be alert when you are visiting other churches in your preliminary planning phases. It will be difficult to mentally escape the example of other worship services, stealing from you the opportunity to create something uniquely yours. I would recommend waiting until you have a working model for contemporary worship before you visit other churches, using the experience to fine tune what you have already created.

Section 6

Hiring and Empowering Worship Leaders

1. Hire Effective Worship Leaders

2. Compensation for Contemporary Worship Directors

3. Titles: The Peter Principle

4. Avoid Co-titles

1. Hire Effective Worship Leaders

All too often, the hiring of a worship leader is more of an audition than an interview. I would encourage decision makers to regard musical talent as a major attribute when hiring a worship director, but there is much more to consider. I've learned that the best musicians are not necessarily the best candidates. Don't get me wrong; there is value in picking the best musicians you can. Good musicians gravitate toward other good musicians. It will be easier to build the band you are hoping to build when your leader is a quality musician. But if that person does not have strong management skills, people skills, organizational skills, and communication skills, your contemporary worship ministry will have limited potential. It's also extremely important the person you select have a good theological grounding. A Master of Divinity may be as useful as an advanced degree in music (I am biased, of course).

Here are some great questions to ask when interviewing candidates: "What is your favorite song?" "Why is it your favorite song?" "Can you explain the lyrics?" These questions probe the candidate's understanding of the music they will be leading.

Also ask your candidates what their favorite Gospel is and why. Their answer will show their investment in knowing Scripture. Ask them to give you song choices for different themes or Scripture. A promising candidate should be able to answer these questions easily and effectively. Playing music is less than half of the work of this job. Your contemporary worship director will spend their week planning, organizing and managing. Relatively little time each week is spent actually playing music. When hiring a contemporary music leader, make sure they are capable of handling all of these responsibilities.

Your candidates should be able to play guitar or keyboard or both. Keys can be used in a wide range of styles from ballads to funk. Keys help vocalists connect to a melody. Guitars offer an ideal leadership posture and are portable for all of your off-stage events. Also, because drummers are so rare and valuable, having a rudimentary knowledge of percussion is necessary. The ability to play drums should give candidates a leg up.

Refrain from choosing someone as your director whose only musical qualification is singing. They must have skill as an instrumentalist in order to effectively lead other instrumentalists. Otherwise he or she will likely be dependent on the instrumentalists in the group to create their own lead sheets and essentially lead themselves. This means you would need to create another paid position or be dependent on volunteers for instrumental direction.

2. Compensation for Contemporary Worship Directors

This is not an easy question, and it will need to be answered on a church-by-church basis. Within major denominations, there are usually guidelines for paying staff, and I would encourage your committee to begin there. What we pay our contemporary worship directors reflects our investment in contemporary worship. For example, if you choose to pay your contemporary worship director the same as you pay your traditional worship director, you are communicating that contemporary worship is just as important.

Developing a thorough job description is a good place to begin if you are going to be paying your contemporary worship director a part-time salary. For part-timers, it is unrealistic to expect them to be at every meeting and to be available outside of practice and worship times. If you are paying part time, expect your director to have other primary employment, which will be the priority for them. I would suggest adding office hours to their pay structure. Once you have set the number of hours necessary to do the job, add at least two additional hours a week to their pay and require that your new hire be on-site and accessible during a set period of time each week (office hours) outside of practice and worship.

If your church can afford to pay your contemporary worship director full time plus benefits, you will be able to choose from a national pool of candidates. Full-time contemporary worship director positions are somewhat rare, and you can be very selective if you can afford it.

Be mindful of Equal Employment Opportunity laws. In churches, there are still legal clauses that exempt them from EEO policy. These policies exist for good reasons, however, and make sure your committee does not enter a candidate search with any predetermined notions as to what race, age, gender or sexual orientation they should be. Be prayerful and open to God's leading and select the best candidates based on their merit, trusting the Holy Spirit to guide you.

3. Titles: The Peter Principle

The Peter Principle, in a nutshell, insists that when given a task, a group of people will elevate leaders among them, based on their competence. People will rise to the level of their competency and will be limited to the extent of their incompetency.

In my former career, I worked for a software company that employed the Peter Principle. We didn't necessarily have titles, and we functioned together as a team with some of us taking leadership roles and others waiting for leadership to just happen. The end result is that Type A personalities wound up running the place and Type B personalities wound up following. This structure is idealistic and even adventurous. The downside for us was there was considerable confusion and ultimately way too much decision-making and arbitration at the top tier executive level.

Without titles and without clearly defined authorities and responsibilities, the buck had nowhere to stop until someone with formal executive authority made decisions. In this case, the owner of the company wound up making day-to-day decisions; this took a good portion of his time that could've been used for functions more fitting to his role.

The phrase "you're not my boss" was quite common in our workplace. So, as promising as the Peter Principle may be as a forward-thinking and idealistic strategy, the functional reality of this approach, by not having clearly defined titles and responsibilities, defers way too much authority to anyone with a clearly defined leadership role, which is usually the executive personnel.

Within a church, we see this a lot. When staff members lack clearly defined responsibilities and authority, pastors are left to make way too many decisions. In the role of setting up, maintaining and developing contemporary worship, it is necessary to have staff members who have the freedom to make day-to-day decisions with the trust and confidence of their pastors. It is important that worship leaders have some authority. They need to be able to make decisions with volunteers, the liturgy, song selection, style choices, and so on without having to go through the executive pastoral staff. Titles are very helpful here.

When it comes to worship leadership, there is a huge difference between the words director and coordinator. The title "director" implies you have authority to make decisions within your realm of influence. The title "coordinator" implies that you are facilitating worship instead of leading worship. Give some thought to the titles you give to worship leadership staff so they are equipped with the appropriate authority.

4. Avoid Co-titles

My former pastor, who was a very successful and influential pastor for over thirty years, insisted when he was first called to our church that he not be a co–pastor. He knew that as much as the idea of a pastoral partnership seems plausible and potentially fruitful, it would become a source of tension and dysfunction. I agree and have experienced this tension and dysfunction firsthand. Without a clearly defined leader, inevitably there will be confusion. If you have two leaders with the same title (co-directors, co-coordinators), their strengths and weaknesses will eventually become evident. When there are two people with the same title, competition between your leaders is inevitable, especially when resources become scarce. When you have two staff members with the same title and the same expectations, it's incredibly unlikely there will be an equitable distribution of job responsibilities.

Often, we settle for creating co-positions because we're unwilling to choose between candidates. As much as I would like to celebrate the idealism of setting up a structure based on respect and sharing, the actual business of doing church work requires streamlined decision making.

As an alternative, if there are two candidates who are sharing the same title, it is probably best to make one Director and the other Assistant Director. When you give some thought to what responsibilities each worship leader may have, new and perhaps more creative titles may emerge. I would encourage you to take time to think through what title you assign the people who will be responsible for leading contemporary worship. Thinking strategically about your titles will help streamline communications, execute vision, define expectations, and share responsibilities.

Section 7

Managing Transition

1. Wiser Wolves

2. Consider Displacement

3. Creative Titles

1. Wiser Wolves

One of my favorite stories, which is a parable of sorts, is the story of the "Two Wolves on a Hill." These wolves were sitting on a hill, looking down at some sheep. The younger wolf says to the older wolf, "Hey – let's run down this hill and catch one of those sheep!" The older and wiser wolf then replies to the younger one, "Instead, let's walk down, and get them all."

This parable is good advice for anyone who is looking to either start or renovate contemporary worship. There is going to be resistance. It's going to be hard. You are going to make some mistakes. Feelings will get hurt. Because of this, it's good advice to have some patience and give a lot of thought to how you proceed.

Once you decide to create vibrant, meaningful contemporary worship, it is tempting to rush into it. When we give into this temptation, we build a false sense of urgency. Take time to consider your decisions from many different angles. It may be better to work in stages.

For example, some churches start by introducing their contemporary services on Saturday evenings. People who are used to a traditional culture feel less put out when the contemporary service is not in competition with their service on Sunday morning. Then eventually they grow to the point where Sunday morning contemporary services made sense, allowing the traditional contingent time to get used to this new thing. Some congregations start contemporary services once a month on Sunday mornings. As their services grow in popularity, they increase it to twice a month. In time, these churches may have contemporary worship every week.

These deliberate transition periods are much more palatable for folks who do not initially see contemporary worship as legitimate. If you are introducing contemporary worship into a potentially hostile environment, a focused incubation strategy may be your best way to limit discord resulting from these changes. Doing too much too quickly builds fast and strong walls between camps that favor different worship styles. Sometimes cultural shifts need to be abrupt, but for most denominational churches, respectfully building momentum is the best approach.

The same is true for new worship leaders who want to reinvent their current contemporary worship. You may want to start by implementing a new song once a week. Over time, the culture, the catalog and the overall vibe of your contemporary worship group will change. Sometimes new leaders have to make architectural changes. For example, contemporary worship may have been led by a choir until you were hired, but you want to transition to band-led music. In situations like this, you can't help but upset the apple cart. New leaders need to be firm but flexible as they institute changes. Good leaders maintain a healthy tension toward positive changes without being disrespectful to the ways and means they are moving beyond.

As you begin setting up contemporary worship, our friends who are carpenters offer some good metaphorical advice: "measure twice – cut once." Take time to get advice, look at decisions from different vantage points, and be prayerful. Most of us will find that as long as we have a plan and a vision for contemporary worship and as long as we are respectful, patient and gracious, we will get there.

2. Consider Displacement

Whenever you start a contemporary service, most likely there will be people who feel displaced. If you are starting a contemporary service from scratch, considerable thought should be given to people who will be asked to change their worship habits. Worshippers are creatures of habit. When our initiatives, as honorable and necessary as they are, force people to do church differently, we must proceed with care and open, abundant communication.

I've witnessed this type of predicament when my church decided to start a 9:00 A.M. contemporary service in our main sanctuary, resulting in the displacement of our 8:45 traditional service. In response, we decided we would renovate our fellowship hall to make it more "worship worthy," and we relegated the 8:45 worshippers to a smaller, less equipped, less formal space. There were hurt feelings and animosity, causing a fracture in the relationship between church members who prefer different worship styles.

In retrospect, we could have taken different steps to make this transition less painful, if not celebrated. We spent considerable money on renovating our fellowship hall, but if we had invested a little more money on building a separate chapel designed primarily with the cooperation of the 8:45 traditional worshippers, we could have built something very special, strategically fit to the needs of that smaller gathering. Such a structure would cost more money at first but would be something that 8:45 worshippers would be more invested in since the space would be custom built for their needs and wants.

Chapels, when done well, can be built in such a way using natural light and wood tones to make a more intimate and more nurturing worship space. Chapels also offer wonderful spaces for weddings and funerals and can be used to generate some revenue. As you consider adding a contemporary worship service, pay attention to anyone or any group who might feel displaced.

When reinventing contemporary worship, it is likely that some volunteers will be displaced as well. The people who execute the current paradigm may become displaced in order to make room for new directions. For example, choirs may not be part of the contemporary music strategy. If the members of that choir are no longer going to be singing every week, special attention should be given to your strategy as to how to make that transition. Displaced choir members will have hurt feelings, but they are more hurt when the leadership team is not direct with them.

It may be necessary to replace instrumentalists, soloists and AV personnel. Also, you will most likely be asking the congregation to say goodbye to a good bit of their current music catalog. Directness, openness and clarity are necessary tools for making these transitions. Change hurts, but we know that pain is part of birth. There's no way you will be able to start or redirect a contemporary worship service without some hurt feelings. These growing pains are necessary, and how you deal with them can have a tremendous impact on the success or failure of your new worship service.

It is necessary to be firm but caring in dealing with people whose roles change as you move forward. Creativity will be your best ally in these cases. For people who are losing their jobs in a particular worship service, be creative in finding new work for them in which they can continue to offer their gifts and continue to feel needed and respected. Never underestimate the personal value volunteers ascribed to their own identities based on their function within worship.

I strongly recommend one-on-one meetings with any person who you suspect feels displaced. Group meetings often cascade into gripe sessions. Group sessions can function as an echo chamber, ramping up emotions, and causing more damage than healing. And it is difficult to address real feelings on a group level. One-on-one meetings over lunch or coffee will provide a much better avenue for discussion and will offer the individual care these situations require.

When bringing in new musicians, it is a safe assumption that the people who were previously carrying out their role will feel somewhat displaced. It's important to convey to these members an understanding that the ministry and its mission is bigger than any individual. Sharing in this ministry should be a goal and having more people involved within this ministry will make it stronger and more dynamic. For folks who will be sharing responsibilities, it's important to remind them that a sure sign of ownership is to be able to share or give away something. Being alert, aware, and proactive about feelings of displacement will serve you well in minimizing hurt as you embrace transition.

3. Creative Titles

A title can mean the world to some staff members and volunteers. Coming up with creative titles can help people feel a sense of purpose, value and accomplishment.

Here's an example of how this works: Once, I had an individual who arguably was not a very good singer. He sang with our contemporary choir for several years. When it came time for us to transition out of having a choir to functioning more as a band, he was displaced. This particular member had some exceptional challenges, making him more emotionally vulnerable than others. Losing the social structure, as well as the sense of importance he gained from being part of the choir, was substantial. As an alternative, I knew this person was gifted in leading prayer. I invited him to become the band chaplain. As chaplain, his responsibility was to lead us in prayer every Sunday morning and to be a prayerful presence at band practice. He was thrilled to have this new role, which he immediately embraced as part of his identity. He was so thankful and did a great job!

Keep in mind that when your task is changing worship, if you break it, you buy it. If you are responsible for displacing staff or volunteers, you must do what you can to re-invest these persons' gifts.

Section 8

Nuts and Bolts – Initial Logistical Concerns

1. Worship Times

2. Naming Your Contemporary Service

3. Bulletins

4. Budgets

5. Copyrights

6. Marketing Strategies

1. Worship Times

I have led contemporary worship services at various different days and times. I have led worship early in the morning, in the evenings, on Saturdays and at 9:00 and 11:00 A.M. on Sundays. I find that the ideal time for contemporary worship in a denominational setting is 9:00 A.M. It is late enough in the morning for families with young children to be there and early enough for older folks to consider it prime time. The time of the morning you have your contemporary worship service really depends on when and for how long your church plans for your education time (Sunday school). Around 11:00 A.M. is when most denominational worship services begin. If your church has only one service on Sundays, it most likely begins between 10:30 to 11:00 A.M.

I would strongly discourage any congregation from displacing its traditional worship service in favor of the contemporary service at 11:00 A.M. One of the churches with which I volunteered switched the 9:00 A.M. contemporary service with the 11:15 traditional service. Members were not happy. The traditional and contemporary worshippers complained — a lot. The research behind the decision was solid, and the strategy was considered growth oriented. But it didn't work. We eventually moved contemporary worship back to 9:00 A.M. and traditional returned to 11:00. Feelings were hurt, members left, giving went down and lessons were learned.

It is not unusual to find contemporary worship services beginning around 9 o'clock. As American families become busier on the weekends, attending an earlier church service is very appealing, especially to those families with children involved in extracurricular activities. Early services are affectionately known as "golfers' mass" or "tailgaters' church."

As much as we who lead worship for a living would like this to not be the case, churchgoers are spending less time in church. They want church to have a profound impact on their families' lives, but they want church to fit into their ever-tightening schedules. Several of the families I know love 9:00 A.M. worship because they need to be finished with church by 11:00 so they can get home, change clothes, have lunch and get to soccer games, cheerleading practice, and the like. Meeting this demographic's needs (young families) is critical to sustaining congregational growth. Worship at 9 A.M. is ideal for helping these families maintain balance with their multiple priorities.

Many churches start their contemporary worship services at 8:30 A.M. The number eight evokes a much different response than the number nine as far as people's assessment of how early something is. When you tell someone that church begins at 8:45 A.M., their response is much more likely to be "that's too early" than if you say church begins at 9 A.M., which feels more like mid-morning in our immediate impressions. When we relegate our contemporary services to time slots before 9 A.M., we are communicating that contemporary worship is not important to our church, or at least not as important as our traditional worship services and our education hour.

I recognize this may sting a little for those of us who have contemporary worship services that begin earlier than 9 A.M., but for the growth and vitality of your contemporary service, 9 A.M. is ideal.

2. Naming Your Contemporary Service

When we name our contemporary services, we add unnecessary parentheses around our worship. Often an assumption is made that named services are just for young people. Contemporary worship, if it is to be effective and inviting, should never be geared or guided to any particular age group. When we use verbs to name our services (Rejuvenate!, Elevate!, Ignite!), we exacerbate the implication that the worship service is only for our youth and that our other worship services will not have the effect of elevating us, igniting us, or rejuvenating us. And if you have an exclamation point at the end of your contemporary worship service's name, it's hard for traditional worshipers to regard it as equivalent to their own.

If you have a traditional service, you wouldn't call it anything other than worship, mass, service or traditional worship. When we name our contemporary services, we relegate those services to a lesser status than our traditional services. We are communicating that we have real worship — traditional — and then something else. Naming our worship services creates barriers. It separates the contemporary worship service from the other forms of worship in your church. Sometimes this is the intention. Most of us, however, want our contemporary services to be considered as legitimate as our traditional services.

Before creating a name for our contemporary service, the question we should ask is this: "What would you name your traditional service?" The idea of naming your traditional service seems silly to most folks. It is silly because you don't have to name it. Traditional worship is just that. I would argue that naming your contemporary worship anything other than "contemporary worship" relegates it to a second-class status in comparison to traditional worship, which doesn't need a crafty name for its recognition. Also, when you name your contemporary worship service, you create somewhat of a closed-ended definition of who you are and what you do.

What we are saying by not naming our contemporary service is that we consider traditional and contemporary worship to be equally valid options. This is a subtle yet bold statement. By not naming our contemporary worship services, we elevate our contemporary worship to the status of traditional worship.

For the band, not having a name helps keep the band itself more open-ended as well. When you have a name for your band, there is an implied boundary defining who is in and who is out. It's been my preference to just call ourselves the contemporary worship team. That name draws in all of the AV personnel as well as the liturgical arts folks. It also inspires people who want to share their gifts in a limited fashion to know that they can participate without being in the band.

Jettisoning a worship service's name may represent a cultural change. Significant thought and artistry usually goes into creating the names for these services. Getting rid of names for our worship services will likely step on toes and hurt feelings, which is unavoidable and unfortunate. If you have inherited a named service, I would suggest seeking out the original creators of the name and talk to them about your interest in changing it. There may be some investments made in logos, printed materials and advertising that will need to be phased out. Be respectful, but be firm, because just as wallpaper can really date a house, a name can really date a contemporary worship service.

3. Bulletins

We live in the Screen Age. Paper is going away, leaving worship planners to ask whether paper bulletins are still necessary. Bulletins do provide a great vehicle for informational handouts and a good source for intra-congregational promotion. But if you are posting this information as well as lyrics on your media screens, the question remains, "Should we go through the work and expense of printing bulletins?" My personal preference is to do away with them to lessen the negative environmental impact of printing hundreds of bulletins soon to be discarded. Going paperless makes a statement about your congregation's environmental stewardship. Bulletins are a staple of modern worship, however, and it may be difficult for many people to let go of them. Each congregation should do its own cost-benefit analysis on using bulletins.

If you decide that bulletins are not going to be used, it's a good idea to have a few mock bulletins drawn up for each service for use by the pastoral staff and worship leaders. These mock bulletins provide an opportunity to recheck the liturgy, song lists, the lyrics, and so on prior to going live. These bulletins help worship leaders know where they are in a service and what's coming next.

In North America, there is a trend toward electronic alternatives to bulletins. There are churches with their own bulletin apps where congregants download the bulletins to their smart phone or mobile device. As an occasional preacher, I can imagine how difficult it might be looking out over a congregation with half of its members looking at their phones. I suspect this is inevitable. Since most of the functions that bulletins provide can be accommodated by your projection screens or other electronic options, give some serious thought to how you might be able to take advantage of them and consider going paperless.

4. Budgets

When I was pursuing my calling into ministry, one of my mentors said half-jokingly that a Master of Business Administration may be as valuable for equipping me for ministry as a Master of Divinity (M.Div). I think about his advice often as I participate in budget discussions. I'm not a financial whiz kid, but I have learned a few principles from more sophisticated money managers when it comes to funding contemporary worship.

First: If you are instituting contemporary worship for the first time, consider a capital campaign to cover startup costs and to build an initial fund from which to draw. The excitement of adding something new should energize giving, especially if you are building. Second: Assuming that you have budgets for traditional worship in place, use those amounts as guidelines for your contemporary worship budgets. Third: Set your budgets for equipment based on input from experts in music production, sound management, and audiovisual. Don't guess. Fourth: Since payroll will likely be your largest ongoing expense, decide early on how you want to staff contemporary worship. Make decisions about whether you want full-time or part-time worship directors and decide whether you want money available to pay instrumentalists and special guests.

Finally, be prayerfully pragmatic. Invest in contemporary worship with a realistic optimism. I'm aware of a church that went all in on contemporary worship that never took off, leaving them with a huge deficit and bitter feelings. Instead, give some thought to a progressive budget with benchmarks based on attendance and giving. This will make it easier to appropriate the needed funds for sustained growth as the contemporary congregation grows. Doing it this way hedges your bets while streamlining decisions to increase the contemporary worship budget as growth warrants.

Here's an example of how this idea works: Let's say you establish a budget of $50,000 a year based on your expectation that contemporary worship will draw half as many people as your traditional service, which has a budget of $100,000. Let's also say you add a clause to your budget that automatically adjusts the budget line annually based on growth. Suppose the contemporary congregation grows quickly, and within a year has as many attendees and is giving as much as the traditional congregation. With that caveat in place, it will be far easier to commit more money based on your pre-established rubric.

If you have had contemporary worship for a while, then you know that considerable money can be spent on nondurable goods. Guitar strings, quarter-inch cables and drumsticks need to be replaced often. Volunteer musicians may offer to cover these expenses for themselves, but these expenses do add up. If you are starting contemporary worship, it's a good idea to have a line item in your projected budgets for miscellaneous expenses. Beyond minor expenses, having a miscellaneous budget can help "spackle the cracks" for your entire AV system.

For example, we had an electrical problem that resulted in our bass player's amplifier getting blown out. It was generous of this musician to use his own equipment and keep it at church for others to use, and it would have been unfair for him to have to foot the $350 bill himself. Having a budget in place allowed us to get the amplifier fixed quickly without holding a committee meeting or the musician paying for it out-of-pocket. These things come up inevitably and having a miscellaneous budget helps us to be prepared.

5. Copyrights

Until a song is old enough to be considered public domain, it is necessary to post any copyright information when using songs that are written by other people. If you have bulletins, the writers and composers of the music you use need to be listed. When you project the lyrics of the song, you must show the writers and composers as well as any pertinent copyright information on screen during song projection. The rules on this issue can be a moving target. We all want to be in compliance with any copyrights.

If it all possible, a conversation with a qualified attorney on this subject is ideal. Attorneys cost money and the likelihood of finding an attorney who specializes in copyright law may be challenging. I suggest you search your congregation for attorneys and ask them to volunteer to help establish your copyright protocols (pro-bono hopefully).

The larger your congregation, the bigger this issue is. If you were to visit a relatively small church, you would be less likely to see copyright information projected at the end of every song. But if you were to worship at Willow Creek in Chicago or any mega-church, rest assured you'll see copyright information with every song.

If there are any events for which you charge admission and you are going to play someone else's music, make sure all copyrights are observed and any royalties are paid. The same is true if you were to create recordings and then sell them. As for sheet music, any copies that are made of purchased sheet music must not be distributed beyond your church. You can make copies, but they need to be kept in house.

It has been my experience that this particular issue is given both too much attention and too little attention. The mere mention of anything legal inclines some of us to overreact to the possibility of being culpable for copyright infringement. At the other end of the spectrum, we see a complete disregard for copyrights. As unlikely as it is that a congregation would be fined for copyright infringement for using popular songs, it's important for artists to recognize other people's work if for no other reason than professional courtesy.

Be sure to discuss copyrights in your initial conversations when starting up contemporary worship. I would suggest designating a person to function as a compliance specialist to monitor the fair use of licensed intellectual property at your church.

6. Marketing Strategies

While you are in your planning phase for contemporary worship, some energy and time should be spent on how you will market your new worship service. Consider the costs of printed materials, advertising, and other items as you earmark budgets for such things. I would advise waiting on launching a promotional campaign until you are up and running. Once you have established what your contemporary worship will look and sound like, it will be easier to honestly promote who you are.

The most effective advertising for church growth is word of mouth. When church members feel compelled to share the worship experience at your church with their friends, it sets a tone for new potential members that commercial advertising cannot produce. Visitors who are invited by members are far more likely to stick around. So when discussing marketing strategies, begin by testing the energy level of your congregation. Try to build excitement in house about what you are doing as a church and what you are working on by installing contemporary worship.

Beyond word of mouth advertising, you may want to use print and electronic media to promote your new or updated worship service. A guideline for advertising is to keep it simple. Try to use as few words as possible while still effectively communicating your vision, mission and hope for worship. I've seen worship services try to describe themselves with multiple paragraphs in their marketing materials. This may be okay in a tri-fold handout, but for any advertising that is to be posted publicly, keep it simple and effective.

Have conversations in your planning committees to decide what words best describe and promote worship at your church. To guide these conversations, ask the question "Can you describe for me a great experience in worship?" Then try to summarize the responses in single words or phrases. These words and phrases can be used in your advertising. Next, ask the question "Can you describe a negative experience in worship?" Work to summarize the responses to words or phrases, and for each one ask "What is the paradox?" Then use those words and phrases. The answers will inform not only your marketing strategy but your overall vision for worship.

Obviously, to grow in numbers, you will need to bring in new people to your congregation. When we create contemporary worship, often we make the assumption that the service should be edgy or extreme in an attempt to appeal to younger folks. Don't fall into that trap. The surest way to get younger folks to disregard your marketing efforts is to pretend to be something you are not. Likewise, it is important to realize that young folks do not want to be caught, so don't chase them. They don't want be sold, so don't try to sell them. Instead, let your marketing reflect who you really are. Figure out what you are proud of in your church, and then use that in your awareness campaigns. Embrace who you are with pride.

Too many churches are using marketing that suggests their worship offerings are juxtaposed to older definitions of church. They use phrases like "worship for people who hate church." If you are doing this, just stop! Church is a good thing. Traditional worship is a good thing, contemporary worship is a good thing. Religion is ultimately a good thing. Celebrate that goodness. Avoid tearing down traditional forms of worship as a means of drawing out how rad you are. Learn to stand on your own merits and resist the temptation of criticizing others in order to define yourself.

The millennials who are my friends desperately want to connect to a sense of purpose and calling. They are not interested in church so much for what it is, but for what it does. The more involved your church is in promoting justice and serving the community, the more appeal you will have with young adults. Let your marketing reflect these commitments and accomplishments, and you will recruit people who will continue that mission.

Section 9

Sacred Space

1. Thin Places

2. Seating Arrangements

3. Small Congregations in Big Spaces

4. Screen Placement

5. Media Projection Software Packages

6. Flooring

7. Build Green

8. Unconventional Venues

1. Thin Places

I've been to St. Patrick's Cathedral in Ireland. I have stood on the edge of Mirror Lake in Yellowstone. I watched the sun go down in Yosemite. I watched the dew settle in Cade's Cove. I have stood in the pulpit at Riverside Church in New York. I had a beer in the pub where Dietrich Bonhoeffer and Paul Tillich used to write theology. I've played Kurt Cobain's guitar in New Orleans. I've knelt at the grotto at Belmont Abbey and privately worshiped at Señora Martha's humble home in Nicaragua.[49]

I love to tell the stories of the times where I stood on sacred ground. And in those moments, I felt a sense of transcendence. These were all thin places for me. I felt closer to God. As worship leaders, it is our privilege and our responsibility to build an awareness of God's transcendence into the spaces we use for worship. Certainly we can fall back on the Scriptural axiom "where two or more gathered...," but we can take it a step further. Without becoming indulgently sentimental, we should build a sense of wonder and embrace the space where we come together to worship as holy ground. It is our job to make our worship spaces as thin as possible.

This can be challenging in contemporary worship. In many denominational settings, contemporary worship is kept separate from traditional worship by relegating it to auxiliary meeting places. Contemporary worship rings out through fellowship halls, gymnasiums and multipurpose rooms throughout the denominational landscape. This is so for many reasons. Probably the best reason for this is that there is another worship service happening at the same time in your main worship space.

Sometimes our primary worship spaces don't have the equipment, utilities, the acoustics, or the space to accommodate contemporary worship. For whatever reason, if your contemporary worship happens somewhere else other than your main sanctuary, it's important to build a sense of sacredness for that space. To help facilitate this, determine what symbols of the faith are important for worship. You may decide that a cross is necessary for centering the room. You may decide that having no religious symbols at all creates a more open-ended, abstract depiction of God's vastness. You may choose traditional symbols from your faith heritage, or you may choose to create all new symbols that reflect a more vivid representation of who God is and what God does.

Once when the worship team I was leading moved into a new space we just built, we had a stage set up for the band, but no cross. There was no altar, there were no banners, just a stage with musical equipment and multimedia. One person came up to me and said, "it feels like we're worshiping a drum set." I had to laugh, because she was absolutely right. Religious symbols are necessary in targeting our focus during worship. Once we installed a cross in our worship space and added a good size altar, it felt more like church.

Symbols often capture some of the mystery we seek to connect with during worship. I recognize there is a significant movement in contemporary worship to reorient ourselves to different symbols that do a better job of telling Jesus's story. I also concur wholeheartedly that there is way too much emphasis on the death of Jesus versus the life of Jesus in our symbols. Without any such symbols, however, our focus will land somewhere and for us apparently it was the drum set. There may be a better symbol other than the cross that can be used as a center of focus in our worship spaces, and I would encourage exploration. For me, the cross is vitally significant both culturally and theologically. If you are setting up your worship space and want to avoid feeling like you are worshiping the band, give serious thought into symbols and their locations so that your congregation's focus is appropriately centered.

Lighting is also an important consideration when setting up symbols in your worship space. How you light the cross, the altar, or whatever liturgical symbols you have can dramatically affect their impact. Effective lighting in general can do wonders for facilitating a sense of sacredness. Lowering the lights can bring focus to the events that are occurring; raising the lights brings awareness to the community that is gathered. Work at striking a balance between the two and be deliberate on how you want to light the room.

It's important to communicate that this space is sacred. If you're conducting contemporary worship in a room that has multiple functions like a gymnasium or fellowship hall, it's easy to lose a sense of sacredness, knowing the meaning of that space is co-opted by other less worship-oriented events. Remind your congregation that all the events happening in that space are sacred. Events like sharing meals, youth ministry or local community events, for example, can be celebrated for their sacredness.

Finally, help your congregation understand the difference between reverence and sacredness as it pertains to your worship space. I'm sure books can be written on this distinction. For a quick definition, I would conclude that sacredness exists regardless of what we do, where reverence is defined by how we respond to sacredness. Holding something sacred and being reverent are not necessarily the same things. The best way to draw this out is to look at the opposites of those terms. The opposite of sacred is profane. The opposite of reverence is irreverent. I think it's quite possible to be irreverent without being profane. Irreverence can often apply a healthy tension and even poke holes in our sense of self-importance. It can serve as a function in helping us not to take ourselves too seriously. Being profane, however, is disrespectful and deliberately intends to offend the sensibilities of those who are seeking to assign sacredness to a place or an event.

For example, applauding the children's choir for a job well done may be slightly irreverent, but is nowhere near profane. Using harsh adult language in a sermon for the sole purpose of shock value with little to no theological grounding is arguably profane. Making the distinction between irreverent and profane may not always be as easy as these examples, but these examples can function as a guideline for making that determination. When we understand the difference between irreverent and profane, we better understand reverence and sacredness, allowing us to fully embrace the sacredness of our worship even if it is considered irreverent.

Work to lead your congregation in understanding that the relaxed nature of contemporary worship may, in some cases, be considered irreverent but should never be considered anything less than sacred.

Finally, as we embrace new ways to collectively praise and commune with God, avoid worshiping worship and realize that how we worship has changed dramatically over the centuries and will certainly continue to evolve. The task of creating thin places, creating worship spaces that optimize opportunity to sense and be reminded of God's presence should be an ongoing endeavor. Once you have established your worship space, it is important to evaluate it with some frequency, adapting it to your congregation's ever-changing needs.

2. Seating Arrangements

In contemporary worship or any worship service you may be building from scratch, you have an opportunity to be creative with your seating arrangements. There is a lot to consider when it comes to seating. First, let's talk about comfort. When making decisions on purchasing seats, make sure you pick seating that is comfortable. Try sitting in the chairs you are considering for at least 45 minutes before investing in them. Have people with different body types try the chairs or pews before you spend money on them.

At a church I served, we met in the gym and used folding metal chairs with just some moderate cushioning. Even though I was a younger and reasonably fit guy, I struggled to sit in those chairs for more than 25 minutes. The chairs themselves created a limitation to our growth potential. Only people who could physically tolerate those chairs would join, sharply constraining our available growth demographic.

Next, I strongly recommend purchasing chairs that can be stacked and moved in, out and around your worship space to allow for different events. Take some time to configure your seating arrangement itself. Pointing all of the chairs toward the stage/altar heightens focus on the liturgy. Setting the chairs up in the round heightens a focus on community. Linear, row-by-row pews are giving way to less rigid seating arrangements. Over the years, I have developed a profound preference for worship in the round. Being able to see other worshippers' faces creates a conversational feel, changing worship from a didactic tone to more of a dialectic one. Worship ergonomics can substantially affect a worshipper's experience.

Finally, time should be spent on figuring out the best arrangement for seating as to maximize functionality and efficiency during worship. For example, you want to have a communion game plan before deciding where the chairs or altar might go.

3. Small Congregations in Big Spaces

When I was fresh out of college, I worked as an assistant manager at a grocery store. I learned a lot about merchandising. I learned that you sell way more product if the displays are nice and full. Full displays are inviting and compelling to customers. When our product displays were sparse and spread out, we sold far less merchandise.

A similar response happens when our worship space is either full or sparse. I find it's easier to grow from 200 to 300 people than it is to grow from 100 to 125 in the same space. When your worship space seems full, there's an energy that fuels your worship service. When a good number of people attend and seating becomes scarce to latecomers, there is a buzz that is compelling and inviting. When you're at 85 percent occupancy in your worship space, you are full. There's a tipping point where people will choose other worship services if they feel like they are too crowded. So if you're blessed with 85 percent occupancy, it may be time to add additional seating, possibly additional worship services or build a new building.

At the other end of the spectrum, if your space is way too big for the number of people who come to worship, the folks who do come often feel disconnected from other congregants. There is a ghost town feeling that dampens the energy of your worship experience. If this is the case, try sectioning off your worship space so that the people who come to worship sit closer to each other. This way they can hear each other singing and can feel more together during the service.

I've seen this strategy work. By feeling more connected to each other, there was a better vibe during worship and attendance increased. As months passed, the reserved ropes used to partition the worship space expanded outward until they were no longer needed. I attribute this success story to what I believe is the primary motivator for us to come to church. I believe we want to come together and be in each other's presence while we celebrate God's presence among us. We come to worship to be closer to God and to be part of a community. The feeling of community we have when we worship is dramatically affected by our proximity to each other.

If you have two separate worship services in the same space that happen at different times and both have low attendance, I would strongly encourage you to combine those services. It will be painful at first for those who give up their preferred worship time, but the feeling of worshiping together in communion with a larger congregation will ultimately win out. With a fuller worship space, you give yourselves a significantly better posture for growth.

4. Screen Placement

In contemporary worship, multimedia is a huge part of making song lyrics, announcements, videos and PowerPoint presentations accessible to congregants. The locations of these screens should take some serious thought. You must consider height, clarity and direction of your screens, as well as how many you will need. Consider natural as well as unnatural light when setting up the screens. If you have natural light in your worship space, it will affect your multimedia projection.

Multimedia is fundamental to most contemporary worship services. Some would say, myself included, that it is mission-critical. The problem with multimedia for many congregations is cost. Projectors and screens can be quite expensive and may be cost prohibitive. You may decide that adding multimedia is to be done in stages. Whatever the strategy is, you want to receive the most out of this significant investment and should consider the following:

First, consider height. Screens should not be so low they are obstructed by ministers, musicians or church fixtures. Likewise, they should not be so high up that you have to stretch your neck to look at them. I would suggest trying some mock placements. Use ladders and bed sheets to emulate possible screen positions for your committee to review. The mock placements should be tried with sheets that are roughly the same size as the screens you are thinking about installing. Also, consider the location of the projectors. Typically they are up high or even behind the screens to prevent the light they project going directly in someone's eyes. When considering placement, think about how many screens you will need. During your mock setup, have people of different heights and ages sit and stand at different locations in your space to evaluate where the screens should be. If you find that one side of the room has to stretch too far, two screens may be necessary.

Second, consider screen clarity. Different screens and projectors have different costs associated with them. Clarity is the main variable that affects price. Decide first what level of pixel clarity is necessary. You may decide all you need is basic legibility, making a lower priced projection system a possibility. You may want more clarity for projecting videos for sermons, movie night for the congregation, VBS video, and the like, which would require a higher degree of clarity. You may also want to add a wow-factor by using hi-def projection. When pricing technology, there is usually a sweet spot. That means wherever you find yourself in the evolution of video projection, you should be able to afford better than bottom of the line, basic equipment with a little more investment. But you can save a money by avoiding top of the line, cutting-edge equipment.

Next, the direction the congregation faces should be considered. For congregations that have screens in the center of the worship stage/altar area, this is not much of an issue. If they are right or left of center, consider congregational worship ergonomics. The main issue with screens that are centered is they are often in competition with other liturgical elements or symbols. Before placing screens, see if they will impede or replace meaningful symbols. If they do, consider options such as two screens, one on each side, or a remote drop-down screen in the center that will temporarily cover a central cross or some other symbol.

Lastly, consider light. If you place screens near windows, consider the impact of the light on your projection. When trying mock set ups, I would encourage you to test them during the time of day you would normally be having worship. Remember that different seasons can affect the amount and direction of the light in your worship space, which of course affects the screens. If the natural light in your worship space does interfere with projection, consider ways to shade the natural light or consider alternate placement of the screens. This may add to your budget, so know before going in whether you will need to address these issues. If the light in the room competes with the screens, you will need strategies for dimming while projecting.

A quick word on light: a common complaint among contemporary worshippers is that we make it too dark in the worship space in order to make projection clearer. They say it is difficult to see and interact with fellow worshippers, and it feels like a movie theatre. Natural light is a wonderful symbol of a loving God and should be preserved if possible. With this in mind, try to strike a healthy balance with natural light and screen clarity. LED screens, which can be extremely expensive, do address the issue of light wash on your screens. As prices for LED screens continue to drop, consider them a first option if the cost is comparable to screens and projectors.

5. Media Projection Software Packages

If you have a multimedia system in place, you're probably already using some form of media tool like PowerPoint or SHOUT media. These utilities make it easy to manage a worship service. If you don't have software that helps project lyrics, announcements, sermon notes, and so on, it may be worth your while to investigate some of these programs. This software can be quite pricey, so serious thought should be given to how you want to manage the media of your multimedia system.

There are a few things you would want to consider when choosing a media production program. First, and I think foremost, is user friendliness. The most difficult participants to find in contemporary worship (besides a drummer) are qualified AV people. An intuitive media projection program makes it easier to train new volunteers who may not have advanced computer skills. User friendliness certainly increases the value of a media projection program.

Have your team evaluate demos of whatever software you may be considering. Also, think about what your needs are for multimedia. If all you need are lyrics projected on the screen, PowerPoint or Keynote work quite well and are relatively inexpensive compared to most media projection software packages. Media projection is an incredibly valuable tool in contemporary worship. It could be used not only to project lyrics for songs but to play videos during sermons or in lieu of sermons. You can use multimedia to project sermon notes or elements used in sermons such as bullet lists or Scripture for reference.

In one of the churches I worked in, we had a separate projector that shown against the back wall behind the soundboard so band members could read lyrics while singing. This kept our noses out of our music stands, kept our heads upright, which is ideal for singing. Pastors can take advantage of back wall projection to post their sermon notes so that they don't get bogged down looking at their paper notes.

Media projection unlocks a number of possibilities. Having a good media management tool may be well worth the investment for your church. I won't recommend any specific programs out there. Instead, I would suggest your team review at least three different kinds of software before making a selection. A simple Internet search for church media projection software should reveal a good list from which to begin working.

6. Flooring
Since music is a focus of contemporary worship, flooring should be considered as part of your comprehensive acoustic strategy within your worship space. Warm, earth-toned carpet

works well. Hard surfaced flooring (basically anything that needs to be polished) is cold and clinical, and it drives sound techs nuts. I highly recommend low-maintenance, commercial carpet tiles. These are great in case of bad spills. The carpet tiles can be pulled up and replaced with some ease.

If your contemporary worship space is in a gymnasium or some other multi-purpose room, consider gym carpet, a low profile carpet that allows for activities while providing a warmer, better sounding environment. While we are on the subject of flooring, by all means allow congregants to have coffee in the worship space. Think of your worship space more like a den and less like a formal sitting room. Don't worry about stains and such on the carpet; they can be easily fixed. A cold and forbidding worship environment is a lot harder to remedy than a stain in the carpet. Making our worship spaces inviting and comfortable starts from the floor up.

7. Build Green

If you are blessed with the resources to build or remodel a space for contemporary worship, strongly consider building green. Natural light, geo-thermic heating and cooling, energy-efficient materials, recycled materials, responsible-use plumbing, solar panels, and the like all help create a statement of responsible stewardship. Taking care of creation is a way of honoring God. By building or remodeling green, we are communicating that we care about sustainability and respect the gift of creation.

8. Unconventional Venues

Your church may have decided to start a contemporary service, and you are thinking about building a new space for it. Perhaps you have one, but it has outgrown its space. Perhaps you are considering a satellite church or a mission church with a contemporary focus. If any of these apply, one option to consider is using local music venues on Sunday mornings. Several churches rent high school cafeterias or auditoriums. These venues are decent due to the already present chairs, electricity and in some cases, stage lighting and multimedia.

You may be able to work out an arrangement with a local bookstore or coffee shop for a smaller, more intimate option as a worship venue. On a larger scale, music venues with sophisticated sound systems and lighting systems normally can house plenty of chairs and/or tables. These establishments can hold hundreds of people and usually have sufficient available parking nearby. Music venues (night clubs) are rarely open on Sunday mornings, so any money the venue makes in rent during this time is a win for them, especially if you work out a cleaning arrangement in lieu of rent.

Many of these venues also have sizable kitchens to accommodate meals or at least coffee. If you can work out an arrangement to charge for coffee or soda, music venues stand to make a small profit while providing a comfortable atmosphere for worship. Owners of local music venues may be entitled to some tax benefits for partnering with your church as well.

At the time I am writing this, I am aware of a few churches like this. *Imago Dei*, which is located in Greenville, South Carolina, comes to mind. Their church meets at a local restaurant/tavern/venue called The Handlebar. I was doing some work with the band members of Jars of Clay who were playing there on a Saturday night. After their set, we cleaned up, cleared out and set up for worship in the morning. I remember thinking, "This is just so cool! And so practical!"

When considering a venue for worship, whether you are building, remodeling, borrowing, renting or bartering, think about what physical accoutrements are needed and never forget it is the presence of God that makes a place sacred. Remember to invite God to be the center, the focus and the purpose of all you do. Where you do worship is always less important to why.

♪♪♩

Section 10

Contemporary Liturgy

1. Flow of Service

2. Gathering Music and Countdowns

3. Respect the Sacraments

4. Preference versus Sacredness

5. Singing the Liturgy - Confessions and Creeds

6. Liturgical Dance

7. Centering Time

8. Use Silence in Worship

9. Know When to Speak Up

10. Sensory Worship

11. Postludes

1. Flow of Service

Worship leaders are responsible for discussing and deciding how your contemporary service will flow or how you will include all of your elements in worship and in what order. There are several common approaches you can use as models. It is common for contemporary worship services to front-load their music, playing four or five songs in the beginning of the worship service, followed by announcements, Scripture reading, sermons, prayers, and then one or two songs at the end. This format works for some congregations, but I would not recommend it. As we strategize about the way our worship service flows, it's important to consider the ever-shortening attention spans of our congregants.

Aspiring preachers learn in seminaries that they will start losing people's attention if their sermons exceed 20 minutes, if not 15 or 10. It is a challenge to keep our congregations mentally invested in our progressively kinesthetic culture. Using music to create ebbs and flows within the service may be an effective way for you to keep your congregation's attention.

Here's an example of liturgical format that flows in a way I've grown fond of. Begin with a very brief welcome, then two songs for gathering music, announcements, centering time in prayer, opening song, children's message, Scripture reading, sermon, message song, sometimes communion, prayer, sending song, postlude. This format ensures we don't spend too much time in music or too much time talking. Music works to break up the service.

I like to plan the songs and liturgy in such a way that there is an hourglass design to our service, placing the higher intensity, more participatory songs and events at the beginning and end of the service, while leaving the middle for lower intensity, less participatory events. The songs we play have different levels of intensity. There are intense congregational songs, and at the other end of the spectrum we have more introspective songs.

I like to have the strong congregational songs in the beginning and certainly at the end of each service. I prefer to use the quiet more introspective songs toward the middle of the service. During communion it's important to not blow the doors off the place with a loud, upbeat song. Instead, quiet songs with softer instrumentation do a better job of facilitating the prayerful, contemplative moment that best accompanies communion.

Occasionally altering the flow of your service on special occasions can communicate something to your congregation in and of itself. For example: on All Saints Sunday, it works well to start with quiet, more contemplative songs. Then as the service moves on, increase the intensity and the optimism of the songs you use, closing with the song that speaks to the hope of the Gospel message. On All Saints Sunday, we have a dual responsibility of creating space for us to mourn those who we've lost and have equal responsibility in celebrating those lives by finding joy and hope in the reality that death is not the end. By guiding the flow of the service, we effectively meet both tasks.

Here's another example: On Palm/Passion Sunday, we can set the flow of the service in the other direction. Start with joyful and triumphant songs to celebrate Palm Sunday, then work through the service with progressively more contemplative songs, ending with a solemn a capella piece for a sending song. Do this to emulate the transition from the joy of Palm Sunday to the sorrow and shared anxiety of the Passion. Through the flow of our service, we are able to tell the story of Palm/Passion Sunday in a more vivid and creative way. This, of course, sets the table for Easter the following week.

One last note on flow: consider the logistics of your musicians moving into position and transitioning to and from their seats in the congregation. You want to minimize dead air, so insist that your musicians set their printed music up prior to worship. Also, try to couple the movement of your musicians on and off stage with the movements of other events.

Use elements such as the passing of the peace, children's messages and communion as opportunities for transitioning to and from the stage or whatever location from which you offer music.

2. Gathering Music and Countdowns

When does your service actually begin? My experience is that worshipers in general consider the official beginning of the service to be when a pastor or someone official starts talking over the microphone. Many of us use gathering music while people are coming in, finding seats and preparing for worship. Those of us who have been doing this for a while know there will be significantly more people in your congregation by the time you finish gathering music than when you start, and that's okay.

I've seen several contemporary worship services use a countdown. Typically, these countdowns are projected on their screen, letting the congregation know exactly when worship will begin.

There is a functional convenience to this strategy in that it keeps the band, the clergy and the congregation all on the same page and makes sure your service starts on time. I would not, however, recommend using countdowns in general. There's something inorganic about using a countdown to begin worship. It's rather abrupt and frankly not geared for adults. Not to mention, the practice of using countdowns has run its course as a new idea for worship. Several of the worship leaders who I've met with previously used countdowns, but they have decided they have outgrown the idea.

If you are using music for your gathering time, I found that two songs are plenty. You don't want to task your music group with having to prepare several songs that over half the congregation will not hear. So for the first gathering song, I have traditionally used the same song that will be the closing or sending song. This means one less song to prepare and an opportunity to teach the song to the congregation before it is played at the end of the service. For your second gathering song you can play something that leads into your theme of the day, allowing your pastors a convenient jumping-off point. We've experimented with doing three or even four songs during gathering, but two songs have proven to be ideal.

3. Respect the Sacraments

One of the advantages of contemporary worship is the flexibility to add to, subtract from, or modify our approaches to sacraments. Traditional worship in denominational settings is a bit more scripted, and there are more rigid expectations of how the sacraments should be administered. Many of us in denominational settings have used the flexibility found in contemporary worship to make meaningful changes to the words and practices surrounding the sacraments. Give some thought to the words and elements you use and your methods of distribution.

For example, one of the churches I've visited offered a "laying on of hands" when receiving bread and wine. They had teams who met you once you've received a wafer and wine (in this case I used intinction). These teams gathered around you in a small huddle with arms around your shoulders. There they prayed for you, offered a hug and then sent you back to your seat. It was one of the most powerful communion experiences I've ever had. Similar adjustments can be made to baptisms, creeds, confessionals or any of the other liturgical elements employed in your worship services. Members of your congregation may struggle with any changes made to the way you administer the sacraments. Before making any changes, decide as a church what works for you and proceed respectfully, with purpose.

If there are traditional liturgical elements you have not done in your contemporary worship for a while, consider adding them in on occasion. For example if your traditional worship services offer a time of confession and absolution, but you don't observe that practice formally in your contemporary worship services, adding a confession on occasion may be powerful for those who have not done it in a while. The point to be considered here is that contemporary worship should be flexible enough to include the traditional elements it moved away from originally. Contemporary worship is not defined by the absence of traditional elements but by the creative, purposeful inclusion of meaningful experiences.

4. Preference versus Sacredness

When we talk about liturgy in our congregations, it is difficult to find complete consensus. Some people become worked up when you suggest changing liturgical practices to which they are accustomed. This is nothing new. If you are just starting a contemporary worship service and are discussing liturgy, brace for impact. Some folks will argue with you, challenge your decisions, and they may consider your work invalid or illegitimate.

In worship, we tend to conflate our reverence for traditions with sacredness. It helps to remember that Jesus never attended Christian worship and that Christian worship, although inspired by God, is one hundred percent man-made. Religion is an invention of well intended inspired human beings who use symbols to represent divinity.

What is sacred is determined by the collective consciousness of a congregation. For example, if your congregation agrees that celebrating communion each week is sacred, then it is sacred. The problem is there are few things in worship we all agree are sacred. This means that sacredness itself is relative. We are likely to assume that the symbols we hold as sacred are sacred to everyone else, which of course is not the case.

If there is no consensus on what is sacred, decisions are made on preference. Preference is not sacredness. For example, someone may prefer contemporary music over traditional hymns. They may feel adamant about this preference, but they cannot make any claims that their worship style preference is any more sacred than those who prefer traditional hymns. I recognize this situation is commonly played out in vice versa. Either way, we must avoid making our arguments for our preferences as if we have some deeper knowledge of what God wants and deems holy.

A similar problem comes when we want to alter our liturgies. Liturgical elements like communion, confession, absolution, creeds all have Biblical support. These elements also carry a degree of ambiguity as to their meaning from what the Bible doesn't say about them. The correct practice of celebrating sacraments, albeit spawn from Scripture, remains a subject of debate among Christians, causing deep divisions. It's easy to blur the lines between preference and sacredness when it comes to liturgical elements. With liturgy and religious symbols, it is best to build consensus and weigh your choices on a spectrum from preference to sacred.

5. Singing the Liturgy

Confessions and Creeds: Contemporary music can be used to creatively express liturgical events. For example, instead of reading a confession, the congregation can sing a song that reflects the contrition of confession, while recognizing God's power to forgive. In Lutheran settings, I've found songs like "White as Snow" by John Foreman useful. Its lyrics, as well as style of the song, invite a deep, meaningful expression of repentance and an earnest act of contrition, helping us comply with the Lutheran liturgical tradition of confession.

For many denominations, it is proper to recite a creed, demonstrating an allegiance to a shared set of beliefs. Music allows us to express these stated beliefs through song. Some songs have a creed in them, and those songs can stand alone as a fulfillment of a denomination's mandate to state a corporate creed. "Manifesto" by City Harmonic is a good example of a song that functions as a creed. Or, you may conclude that the body of songs offered during worship, sung together by the congregation, carry within them all of the tenants of your creed that would otherwise be spoken. You may choose to acknowledge that by singing these songs, we recognize our beliefs, state them publicly, and are bound together under common understanding.

6. Liturgical Dance

Liturgical dance can open up a whole different dimension to worship. Of course, liturgical dance is not exclusive to any one particular worship style. Be it traditional or contemporary, liturgical dance should be considered in your comprehensive strategy for offering worship. As musicians, we do well to appeal to our congregation's sense of hearing. Liturgical dance, however, interacts with the music and appeals to us visually.

The movement of the dancers can help tell the story of the song and may provide an opportunity for deeper engagement during worship. Liturgical dancers can be a group of skilled dancers with extensive training who can pull off complex choreography. Or it could be just one dancer who interprets the music in his or her own way. Liturgical dance could be children who are just trying out their dancing abilities with simple choreographies. Liturgical dance is wide open. There are not many rules here.

Making liturgical dance happen during worship comes with several challenges. Most worship leaders are not skilled dancers. In order to have liturgical dance, you need a leader, someone who can recruit, manage and coordinate dancers. I found out the hard way how challenging it can be to try to manage liturgical dance. For our Christmas Eve service, I wanted to have dancers who would be dressed as angels. All of the angels, it turned out, were girls between the ages of four and eight with one teenager among them. Getting all of them together at the same time was difficult. Getting all of them together to practice with the band was another challenge. I learned several things from this experience, which did work out to be a wonderful event but not without significant stress.

First, I learned to start earlier, especially if you're working with children whose schedules are tighter than most would imagine. By placing practice times further out on the calendar, it makes it easier to gather everyone in one place for a longer period of time. Second, I learned it's very important to involve parents if you're using kids as liturgical dancers. Parental presence helps the kids to stay on task and comes in handy when you need odd jobs done.

Finally, I learned it is a good idea to come up with recordings that match the music they will be dancing to. If the liturgical dancers are dancing to a recording, this is not an issue, but if they are dancing to live music, try to get a recording of your actual musicians so the dancers can use the exact timing of the song. Timing is critical for dancers, and slight variations from the original recording of a song compared to your band's version of it can throw them off.

Another thing to consider is costumes / apparel. Obviously if you have multiple liturgical dancers, you will most likely want them to wear similar apparel. This may present itself as a wonderful ministry opportunity for any seamstresses or tailors in your congregation who are willing to share their gifts.

Liturgical dancers can also be used to facilitate other parts of your liturgy. For example, the angels we had on Christmas Eve helped distribute small electric tea candles to the entire congregation. When the angels came by and handed out these candles, worshippers would then turn their lights on, progressively lighting the room on Christmas Eve. This allowed us to have a candlelight service without the risk of open flames, which was very important for us at that service since we had over 200 curious children.

Consider the possibilities of liturgical dance and see how it may work with your congregation. As a worship leader, it may be easy to conclude that liturgical dance is "not my job." That assessment is fair enough, but all of us want to do the best we can to tell the Gospel story, and liturgical dance can help toward that end. If you can make time to help set up liturgical dance in your congregation, I'm sure you and your church will be very well blessed by it.

7. Centering Time

I discovered the benefits of yoga several years back. Yoga classes usually begin with some time to focus on breathing, to get centered and prepared for progressively challenging poses. In my pastoral counseling practice, I begin every session by taking some time to breathe, thinking about inviting God's presence in with every breath in, and releasing tension and anxiety with every breath out, thus setting the table for a productive session. I found that adding a similar, deliberate moment to our worship liturgy works well to quietly focus our attention on God's presence. We call this moment in worship centering time. It's important to take time to transition in your worship services.

So many of us lead very busy lives. With countless to-dos, we all have a steady stream of things we are thinking about at all times. Taking time to center ourselves helps us focus on the main event – worship.

In one congregation I served, we began worship by playing some gathering music, followed by announcements, and then we would take a deliberate time to be prayerful and to center ourselves as we transition from arriving there to fully being there, inviting God's presence to fill our minds and hearts as we let go of the things that take our focus from God.

At our church, we used the event of lighting the Christ candle for our centering time. This time is begun with an explanation of centering time and then we offered some simple instrumental music and concluded with prayer. Typically we would have a musician who plays the Native American flute. I find wind instruments to be particularly effective in assisting with centering time. Especially considering that we are inviting God's *Pneuma* (Greek for spirit or breath) to fill our worship space, instruments that use breath help convey that message.

From experience, here's what I found does not work: 1. Gregorian chants seemed like a good idea and is consistent with the whole breath motif, but it was just weird. 2. Electric guitars: they can be startling, and ultimately we found them to be disruptive during this contemplative time. 3. Drums: drums set a different mood and can be quite interesting. But we have found that using drums during centering time tends to draw too much attention away from the moment, as we can't help but catch the beat.

A good axiom for music during centering time is to keep it very simple and pretty. Mellow, non-intrusive instrumentation is ideal.

Centering time can be coupled with other liturgical elements, if time is an issue. For example, centering time could conclude with the recitation of a creed. This time could be used as a time of confession, ending with clergy extending absolution.

Ultimately, incorporating a deliberate centering time does wonders to prepare your congregation and officially begin your worship service with open hearts and focused minds.

8. Use Silence in Worship

Mother Teresa once said: "The fruit of Silence is prayer. The fruit of Prayer is faith. The fruit of Faith is love. The fruit of Love is service. The fruit of Service is peace."[50] Psalm 46:10 invites us and challenges us to "Be still, and know I am God." As worship leaders, we do well to provide opportunities for such stillness and silence. As a pastoral counselor, I've learned that silence is a powerful tool for digging deeper into emotional issues. Silence can be uncomfortable. But silence can be very effective in facilitating an exploration of ourselves both emotionally and spiritually. Adding deliberate moments of silent worship, prefaced by skillful guidance, gives members of your congregation an opportunity to deepen their awareness God's presence and themselves.

9. Know When to Speak Up

I have been blessed to have plenty of opportunities to visit other churches and observe a number of different contemporary worship services. There are so many great subjects to talk about with each experience, but I want to focus for a moment on something I have seen in a good number of these services that should be addressed. All too often in the services I visited, the contemporary worship leaders, who are not necessarily pastors, felt a need to do a whole lot of talking. Some of them felt compelled to explain every song they play, creating a sense that they were trying to sell the song choice to the congregation. Several times I witnessed worship leaders giving mini-sermons in between songs, and frankly, it was tedious. A word or two about the song can be appropriate and sometimes necessary, but talking should be at a minimum.

We expect our pastors to speak with a prophetic voice. Words matter when considering liturgies and sermons. Preachers slave over sermons, often choosing to cut good content for the sake of time. Preachers do what they do with training, skill and talent. The words pastors use are thought out, planned and have purpose. So, worship leaders, if you're going to talk about the songs you are offering, be sure to clear what you are going to say with your pastors. (I have a sense that pastors all over the country will be mentally high-fiving me as they read this.) Make sure everyone is on the same page. Know that the voice you have as a worship leader is amplified, both literally and figuratively, and be thoughtful and intentional with what it is you have to say. Remember that people who write sermons typically spend hours each week in preparation. My homiletics professor advised us to spend one hour in preparation for every minute of sermon.

A similar guideline should apply for worship leaders who are going to be talking about the songs they offer. Remember: if a song you chose requires too much explanation, it probably is not a good fit. Finally, I have never heard a complaint about a worship leader not talking enough during worship. I have on several occasions heard the opposite.

10. Sensory Worship

A few years back, I helped some friends from Wake Forest University start a new worship service. Our purpose was to provide worship that was engaging for all people, regardless of ability. One of our leaders has a child with exceptional challenges. Using her experience, we geared our worship service so that persons who don't use words as their primary means of communication could be more fully engaged.

This type of worship is called sensory worship, which places an emphasis on evoking the Gospel message in creative ways. Of course we use music to appeal to our congregation's sense of hearing. To engage the congregation's sense of touch, we had several hands-on activities. We would dress up sometimes, inviting the individuals attending to be active role players in the Scripture-based dramas we played out. Our prayer time included motion and hand-holding to engage our senses of sight and touch. There were always things to eat at the service, engaging our senses of taste and smell.

We were very visual in how we approached our liturgy, using icons instead of words on our screens and bulletins, helping congregants who cannot read to know where we were in the service. We found this style worship appeals to persons with special needs. Most importantly, parents and caregivers of children with exceptional challenges found a space that was comfortable, inviting and not disrupted by random utterances. In fact, we invited the congregation to make joyful noises throughout.

One parent approached me in tears saying it was wonderful to have a worship service where she didn't feel like she had to apologize for her son's outbursts. Creating a worship space that's inviting to all of God's people should be every worship leader's goal. Sensory worship broadens and amplifies the ways in which we tell the Good News.

As a worship leader, you may want to consider a specific service that goes out of its way to accommodate persons with exceptional challenges. Likewise, you may want to consider adding elements of sensory worship to your weekly liturgy. I would encourage worship leaders to have discussions with the pastoral staff about ways to accommodate persons with exceptional challenges. I am aware of some congregations that are threatened by the disruption that exceptional children may cause during worship. I would challenge these congregations and any of my readers to celebrate diversity in abilities within your congregation. Have honest conversations about not only welcoming persons with exceptional challenges but inviting them to fully participate in your worship experiences and your congregational life.[51]

11. Postludes

For most denominational worship services, we will offer postlude of some sort after a final blessing. In the groups I've led, we typically played the refrain from the sending or closing song as the congregation was dismissed. Sometimes, however, we would re-play a musical offering that was very specific to the day's theme. This is usually a fun idea, but just make sure your band is on the same page. Ensure that everyone has their music ready and can quickly transition.

Ideally, your postlude should send your congregation off with a song in their head. Upbeat and singable songs are most effective here unless you are deliberately trying to set a somber tone (Passion Sunday, for example). The postlude is likely to become the ear worm that stays in people's minds, so make sure you choose songs that say what you want to say. Postludes are worth the time we invest in them. I recognize we all try to beat the clock on Sunday mornings, but we shouldn't underestimate the joyful atmosphere created by postludes as the congregation is heading out.

Section 11

Build Your Worship Team

1. Build the Band
2. Locate Musicians
3. Auditions
4. Compensation for Musicians
5. Vocals
6. Develop Youth Talent
7. Mentor Young Musicians
8. Audiovisual Personnel
9. Share Our Gifts
10. Team Building - Cross Training
11. Inertia

1. Build the Band

So you have decided to start a contemporary worship service. Where do you begin? In my opinion, guitars are to contemporary worship what an organ or piano is to traditional worship. Your contemporary worship director should be a lead vocalist and should probably play guitar or keyboards. Just beyond them, I would start with finding a drummer. Drummers are a special breed and are difficult to find. Good drummers are born, not made. I am an accomplished musician, but I can't play drums. I've tried to learn, and like Tiger Woods' golf swing, becoming a good drummer is beyond my ability.

Drummers are crucial to the sound and atmosphere that contemporary worship is capable of providing. Drummers bring energy and vibrance to your music. They move us in ways other instrumentalists cannot. Drummers add dynamics to our songs and make us dance. And once you have found a drummer, find another one. Percussionists define contemporary worship. By providing a beat, drummers allow your congregation to feel music in some meaningful ways. Having a beat gives congregants another avenue of engagement. I would go so far as to say that without a drummer, you are not there yet in contemporary worship.

Once you have your drummer, the next piece to have is either a lead guitar player or keyboard player. Then you will need a bass player. If you have a talented bass player in your band, consider yourself lucky. A talented bass player can catapult the music you make to a much higher degree of excellence. No disrespect to bass players, but bass players can be made if you just can't find one.

Teaching bass to young people in your congregation is a great ministry in and of itself. The reality of many worship and praise songs is that they are, in several cases, four or five different notes altogether. This makes it possible for young people to be taught how to participate on the bass rather easily. Also, if you have more than one guitar player, one of them can switch to bass. Again, if you have a talented bass player, that's going to open doors for you musically. But if you don't have a bass player, just know it is the easiest part of the equation to accommodate. Younger players can hold down notes on bass with relative ease compared to complex guitar chords that challenge their developing hand strength. The bass can be a great gateway-instrument, inviting young instrumentalists to further their exploration into playing music.

Guitar players, in just about every market, are readily available. In my experience I have never had a shortage of guitar players. As a contemporary worship leader, usually you can have your pick of guitar players. Most bands do well to have an acoustic guitar player and an electric guitar player.

How you proceed with your axe strategy is a decision that should be made before recruiting musicians. For example, if you're going to have a hard rock edge, you want to recruit musicians who want to and can play that style. As for keyboard players, it is true that you can form a band and offer powerful contemporary music without a keyboard; it's just not advisable if you can avoid it. The diversity of music that keyboards allow for should not be underestimated. Keyboards, coupled with players who read sheet music, can quickly provide accompaniment on any ballad and enhance any other songs that you would want to do. So drummers, guitar players, bass players, and keyboard players — this should be your foundation instrumentally.

2. Locate Musicians

Finding musicians can be a daunting task. Of course you want to start within your own congregation. It is never enough, however, to place a notice in your bulletin or write a plug in your announcements, and then just hope people will respond. Taking those steps (bulletins, newsletters, announcements) are an important part of any strategy to find musicians, but rarely will they be sufficient for recruiting the people you need. The principles of networking will be useful in locating people in your congregation who are musicians.

It's more work, but it helps in recruiting musicians who have limited volunteer time available to have a system where someone doesn't have to necessarily be in the band in order to offer their gifts. There should be an open door for your music ministry, as well as a revolving door. This will help with re-cruiting people with busy schedules. It's more work than just having the same five to six people lead worship every week but having many different instrumentalists and vocalists is the best way to add diversity and congregational involvement.

It's common for youth to take interest in contemporary worship. Talk to your youth pastors. Ask them if they are aware of any young people with some musical ability. If you find capable singers or instrumentalists in your youth pro-grams, work with them to create opportunities to learn and serve through music.

If and when you find that you need instrumentalists and vocalists from outside your congregation, there are several places to look. Many cities have a college or university with a music program. Make an effort to know the professors at these institutions and work with them on ways to develop intern-ships. This helps you provide incentive to skillful musicians who are looking to gain experience, as well as college credit. Most cities have high schools that are committed to the arts. If you have such a school, try to build relationships with the teachers and let your church become an avenue for these young musicians to build on their skills and to find an audience.

Also, you could place an ad in music stores to find instru-mentalists. Unlike Schools of Music, finding musicians through music store bulletin boards can be somewhat of a crapshoot. You will need to spend a little bit more time vetting these peo-ple to see if they fit with your designs for contemporary wor-ship. Staffing your band is a continual challenge for worship leaders. Keep a mind-set of recruitment. Always be searching for talent. Be a scout for your ministry and constantly work to-ward connecting people with opportunities to serve and share their gifts.

3. Auditions

Auditions for contemporary worship are uncomfortable and awkward. Worship directors have the responsibility of making sure that the music they pull together is going to be good, while being caretakers of their congregation's gifts. Auditions should focus on musical ability, as well as team unity. Avoid simple dichotomies when auditioning. It's not healthy to decide whether someone is either in or out. If someone is just really talented and/or skilled, then move on to questions about how they see themselves fitting in with your team. At that point you can make informed decisions about moving forward.

When the person auditioning is talented, it's easy. Often we have to make decisions based not on current ability but on potential. Someone may not have the talent or skill to fully participate as a musician in your group, but they may have the potential for developing their abilities over time. With instrumentalists, it's easier to work them in, depending on the difficulty of the songs on which you invite them to participate. For example, my son was learning to play bass. As an incentive, I had him learn a few easier songs and had him play once a month, one song at a time. This peaked his interest and let him develop his skills in order to take on more complex songs. Eventually he started playing more challenging songs and became a regular participant.

With instrumentalists in general, it's difficult to imagine a scenario where you just have to say "no." If someone has an interest in offering their time to play an instrument with your group, you can always try to incorporate them on an as needed basis. Depending on the instrument, you can have other instrument players take a rest every now and then. Or if they're good enough to play an entire set, have them substitute on occasion with the caveat that you provide them a song list way ahead of time so they can work on their own.

For vocalists, auditions can be a whole lot trickier. There's something about singing that makes us very vulnerable. To hear that we're not good enough when we sing can be devastating. When we sing, there is more of a personal investment. Our voice represents who we are on more of an essential level than playing an instrument. So if you're auditioning new potential singers, bear in mind they are taking quite a risk to put themselves out there. If they're not very good, it's best to be honest but caring.

When you are approached by someone who would like to sing with your group, have them pick some solos they would like to lead. I recognize that it may be counterintuitive to start new singers off with solos, but there's method to this madness. By asking them to come in singing solos, you're making it clear you are not trying to fill out a choir. When they audition, if they are good, you have a way to incorporate them within the group. You can tell them that the next time you perform the particular songs that they audition, you'd like to invite them to lead those songs. If their voice is not ready for prime time, however, it will become apparent in the audition. This will provide an opportunity to encourage some coaching to this person who would like to offer their time and energy to your music program. By coaching them, you are essentially saying they're not quite where you need them to be vocally. Then explain to them you don't want to put them into a situation where they won't be happy with the end result.

Depending on what you perceive their ability to be, you may offer an opportunity to sing backup on occasion. To find out if they have the ability to sing backup, start singing a song yourself and ask them to join in with you, preferably with some light instrumental accompaniment. If what they do at this point seems to work, schedule them for at least one Sunday to sing backup.

Just a note on backup singers: unless you have the ability to direct a choir, I would not have more than two designated backup singers who do not also play instruments. If they just don't have the talent, it is your best bet to nip it in the bud. I've had experience with a person who just could not sing and did not play any instruments. This person had a number of challenges and personal problems but a huge heart. He constantly petitioned to be involved in our music ministry, but ultimately I had to be honest with him and let him know that the ability just wasn't there and that it would be irresponsible for me to put him in that position.

As a worship leader, we all face tough challenges we don't expect when we accept these roles. Saying no to this person was one of the toughest things I have had to do, but it was the right call. If you are coming in as a new contemporary worship leader and you have inherited a group, auditions will be very painful. An effective strategy is to first decide exactly what it is you want to sound like. From there, decide what you need instrumentally and vocally, and then meet individually with each of the members of the current team and talk with them about their existing positions.

You may have to ask someone who has been offering their gifts through contemporary worship to stop doing so. This hurts. You will be temporarily very unpopular. Worship leaders with a calling and a vision, however, need an opportunity to execute that vision. When we are called to take over a music ministry, we are expected to bring change. It is difficult to say no, but it is our responsibility when the occasion warrants.

4. Compensation for Musicians

Many churches are blessed with the resources to pay their musicians. Strong arguments could be made to support the necessity of paying musicians. The decision to pay vocalists and instrumentalists for their time and talent should be weighed against several factors. First, obviously, do you have the money? If the answer is no, then move on to the next topic. If you are trying to decide if you should pay your musicians, perhaps consider that typical denominational worship service incorporates quite a bit of music. It is not uncommon for half of the content within a denominational worship service to be music. Certainly we should pay the persons responsible for sermons and our music directors. But what about vocalists and instrumentalists?

It's been my experience that when it comes to music, there are a good number of people who want to share their talents without being paid. There is a beauty in offering these talents free of charge. The Christmas carol "Little Drummer Boy" does a good job of describing just such an offering. But if you have a group that puts in a considerable number of hours of work to provide professional level music, you may find it appropriate to compensate people for their time and talent. Many groups pay only some of their members. As you may guess, this can cause quite a bit of envy and animosity within those groups. In this case, it makes sense to give titles to the musicians you are paying so that the musicians who are not paid understand there is a greater expectation levied on the paid musicians.

Sometimes you will have special guest musicians who require some sort of subsidy. Having a fund reserved for special musicians can be helpful in bringing in outside musicians for special events. It's good to have a reserve of highly skilled musicians who can be called in the event your week to week musicians may be out. For example, a group I managed became completely dependent on having a drummer. Until we built up a reserve of backup drummers, we had a person who would come in and play drums for us for a fee. We were able to contact this fellow at the last minute sometimes. Since he was a session drummer, he was able to pick up our set list with one run through. Obviously, having a fee structure in place with this musician made it easy to call him in when we were desperate. Having paid musicians available to fill in the gaps for your volunteers is a very proactive strategy, allowing for consistent excellence each week.

It is true that you can expect a greater degree of responsiveness and participation from paid musicians, but there are other ways to obtain these results without offering weekly stipends. Motivation is the job of any worship leader. Motivating musicians can be difficult, but you have several tools at your disposal. For example, the musicians with whom I have experience can be very motivated by knowing they are part of something important. I found that musicians become earnestly invested when they truly hold their work as part of their personal ministry, as their primary means of creatively sharing the Gospel. It's a worship leader's responsibility to take time to build awareness of how important the music their group provides is to congregational life and to the life of the body of Christ.

Also, your volunteers can be celebrated and motivated by meaningful gifts. For example, we decided to surprise our percussionist by buying him a new drum. We used money from the church budget and picked it out as a group, without his knowledge. We presented it to him before the entire congregation and asked him to try it out for the first time during worship. You can imagine how much further that gesture went toward making him feel appreciated than just giving him the money.

If you have vocalists and instrumentalists or AV personnel whose gifts and talents you want to celebrate or commemorate, consider making a gift to a particular fund within the church in their honor. If there is a ministry other than music that these people are passionate about, consider making a donation in their honor to it. For example, if you have a vocalist who volunteers time and talent, and you know he/she is very involved in Habitat for Humanity, making a donation in his or her honor acknowledges their gifts shared through music and makes a powerful statement to that person. Such a gesture makes it clear that your congregation values the work they do. For youth musicians, consider creating scholarships or music camp experiences as a means of compensating them for their time and talent. Consider all your options when deciding to pay musicians.

5. Vocals

Without question, this is the hardest part of setting up a band. So many people want to sing in worship. You may decide you want to have a choir in contemporary worship. It's been my experience that choirs in contemporary worship create more of a blended feel than a contemporary one. Choirs do offer some advantages. With choirs, we have the opportunity for many people to be involved at once. Choirs are open-door ministries that allow people with varying degrees of talent to share their gifts. In some cases, choirs make it easier for more traditional-oriented members of the congregation to sing along. If these are your goals, then a choir in contemporary worship may make some sense.

Choirs, however, offer some pretty serious limits as well. First, when hiring or appointing a contemporary director, you will have to limit the pool of candidates to those who have been trained to lead a choir, a skill mostly found in traditionally oriented worship leaders. Next, the overall sound that choirs provide in contemporary worship can border on stagnant. There is not much variance in the overall sound provided by choirs as compared to bands. This means that the musical diversity you may hope to offer could suffer. With choirs, your preparation time goes up exponentially. The time you as a group invest in preparing music will have to be spent on preparing the choir. This will limit your overall catalog of music. Also, using a choir instead of a band will drastically limit the variety of songs you can use in worship.

I think it is important to note that a band is more ecclesiastically evolved than a choir. I have yet to experience a contemporary worship service led by a choir that was formerly led by a band. There are countless bands, however, leading worship in services that were once led by a choir. I have a distinct preference for band-led worship music and strongly encourage contemporary worship leaders to guide their ministries away from using choirs as primary mode of vocal leadership. I recognize that choirs can add power and meaning on certain songs and do recommend bringing in choirs for special songs, especially around the holidays. If your contemporary worship leader is not trained in leading choirs, this may be an opportunity for someone in your congregation who can lead choirs to do so on a limited basis or to get your traditional worship leaders involved in contemporary worship.

6. Develop Youth Talent

There are a number of ways to encourage youth to be involved in contemporary music ministry. Most youth programs have kids with musical skill, AV aptitude, dance or theatrical arts, or other gifts pertinent to effective worship. Involving our youth creates a heightened engagement in worship for younger and older congregants. When your young folks are involved, their families and their friends become that much more interested in worship as well.

Working with youth carries the challenge of working around their typically rigid schedules. Most young people don't have their own means of transportation, so you will need to work with their parents' schedules as well. The logistics of dealing with young musicians can be a headache, but it's difficult to replace the energy and excitement that comes from having musicians who are most likely using their talents for the first time.

Sometimes you may have young musicians who have specialized talents but not much available time. In this case, a good idea is to pick specific pieces of music for them in which they can participate. That way they can contribute their gifts with a limited time commitment. For example, we needed someone to play the flute solo on an original song. We had a young lady who was becoming a competent flautist and invited her to play along with us. Because of her rigorous schedule, she wasn't able to play with us often, but she was thrilled to take part when she could. Consequently, this young lady has gone on to get a degree in music. I like to think her experience with our worship team, albeit limited, helped in her discernment toward that career path.

On several occasions, I've invited college students who were home for holidays and breaks to sing and/or play instruments with our group. I find that reserving preludes (especially around the holidays) for young instrumentalists works wonderfully well. Young people are so excited to share their burgeoning instrumental talents with their church family. Worship leaders should stay aware of kids in their congregations who are learning instruments and then provide opportunities for these new artists to share their gifts.

Working with young people and their parents requires you to plan ahead. Time equals quality. The more advance notice you can give young people and their parents, the more likely you will get better participation. When you're working with young people, there is inevitably a need for more practice time. By planning ahead, you can schedule youth choirs or young guest musicians and have advance notice as to when young people may not be able to be there so you can work around their schedules. Also, when you plan forward, you can meet with young people and ask them what songs they would like to perform. You can leverage their interest by challenging them to work ahead so they can be ready to play these songs well before the entire band practices with them.

For example, we had one young lady who was an incredibly gifted musician. She would have ideas about songs she would like to lead and would let me know about it. Then, looking at the worship schedule, I would find a good week to introduce that song. I wrote it on the calendar and let her know when we were performing it so she could work on preparing the song instrumentally and vocally. When it came time to practice the song with the whole band, she was ready to go. By planning ahead, we do our best to steward the gifts of young musicians.

It is possible, especially in larger congregations, to have an entire band made up of young musicians. Worship coordinators, lay leaders and pastors can function as facilitators more than directors when this is the case. I would strongly encourage having a defined leader or some sort of a leadership presence with youth bands. Youth bands can be very effective, but they need a good bit of care and direction. It is been my experience that youth bands need help focusing and planning. It is a balancing act to provide youth bands with the direction they need without taking over. My advice to anyone responsible for a youth band is to ask a lot of questions, rather than telling them what to do. Then help them follow through on choices they make themselves.

7. Mentor Young Musicians

Helping young musicians develop their artistic skills through worship is a privilege and responsibility. I would go so far to say it is vital to your music ministry to have a constant stream of young musicians offering their talent and developing their skills through your church's music programs. Getting kids involved can be tricky. Certainly the axiom "the rich get richer" applies here. When you have a number of youth who have gone through your music ministries, it sets a precedent, making it easier to attract new youth. If you don't have any young folks coming through your contemporary worship team or you are just starting out, finding the right catalyst to attract participants takes some trial and error.

Here's what does not work: placing a broadcast message in your church bulletin, making a broadcast announcement during worship services, writing blurbs in your church's newsletter. These are all decent ways of making your church aware of a bake sale, but you are unlikely to motivate young people to respond to any of these methods.

Instead, take time and meet with them in their youth groups. Ask them what their favorite songs are and try to get them to play and/or sing them. Keep it light and fun. Ask them if there are any among them who are decent singers. Usually, the group will encourage the ones who can sing to admit it. Then, ask if there's anybody who plays an instrument. My experience has been that the kids who play instruments will let you know if you ask them. Tell them you looking for ways to have more people involved in contemporary worship and that you would love it if any of them would like to share their time and talents in music ministry.

Sometimes you hear kids singing at church. If they sound decent, take that moment to invite them to sing sometime with your contemporary band. Also, keep an ear to the ground for potential instrumentalists. Often in casual conversations, parents reveal that their child is learning to play guitar or piano or another instrument. By following up with those parents and offering an opportunity to play their instrument during worship, you could be providing something to work toward for young instrumentalists.

When there are youth who would like to volunteer in your music ministry, it's important to remember some principles of good stewardship. Youngsters see pastors and worship leaders as authority figures and are predisposed to saying "yes" when they are asked to volunteer. As a good steward, it's important to always have a conversation with their parents to make sure their young folks do not overcommit their time. It's rare that I meet a student who is not involved in multiple activities outside of school, so having a conversation with youthful musicians and their parents about how music ministry will fit into their other priorities is a must. Young people can be incorporated into music ministry in stages. Even if they are involved in worship only once or twice a year, their investment and engagement in worship goes up exponentially.

Getting kids involved in your music ministry can be a great deal of work. The time you invest in them, however, can profoundly change the trajectories of their religious experience. As worship leaders, we have the task of pulling together the best worship experiences we can. It's hard to imagine a better way of adding vibrance and relevance to your worship experience than having an active and consistent program of youth musical development.

8. Audiovisual Personnel

Since multimedia has become part and parcel with contemporary worship, it's very important you have sound techs as well as video projectionists trained and ready. Having a revolving staff and volunteers is ideal for continuity in coverage. I would recommend working with your audiovisual personnel to form a system that allows new volunteers to receive training as well as opportunities to serve. One idea is to have training days. Choose one day each quarter that the current AV staff can conduct training sessions with new volunteers. Promote that training day through your newsletters, announcements, bulletins, website and social media. Ask for new volunteers to sign up for these training days. If no one volunteers, use these training days as time for your AV staff to advance their knowledge and to cross-train each other. Do this until you have plenty of skilled volunteers to cover your AV needs.

9. Share Our Gifts

Contemporary worship provides new and often intriguing ways to share our gifts. By being somewhat more open ended, a wider variety of artistic offerings can be experienced. As Christians, we celebrate the idea that the body of Christ is made up of all of us sharing our gifts and playing our parts. Because contemporary worship offers both traditional and non-traditional forms of artistic expression, it provides an array of opportunities for involvement and the sharing of gifts. For folks who are not artistically inclined, contemporary worship provides ample opportunity to share in worship. For some of us, our contribution to the body of Christ is not preaching, singing, youth leadership or playing an instrument. Instead, some of us prefer to function behind the scenes.

Having gifts of organization, management and vision are important when setting up and maintaining contemporary worship. Finding people with these gifts to work on the various committees around contemporary worship is vital. For example: let's say you have a retired CEO in your congregation who is available for volunteer opportunities. This person is a lifelong traditional worshiper and plans to stay that way. If this person, who knows a great deal about running an organization, were to get involved with setting up and maintaining contemporary worship, they could add an objective perspective to committee decisions along with skillful discernment and vision-based planning. In this example, we see how someone, who would normally not be considered for a role in contemporary worship, can be extremely valuable in its development and continued vitality.

10. Team Building — Cross Training

Back in the 1980s when I was studying for one of my business classes, I noted that the idea of cross-training was gaining momentum in corporate circles. The idea here was to keep employees engaged and challenged with maximum growth opportunity by cross-training on different roles within their company.

As you build and manage a worship team, a similar benefit is available when we teach each other how to do the things we know how to do. For example, if you have someone who is especially good at singing harmonies, have them help other folks who can sing only melodies to try to learn from them. If you have someone who plays guitar, encourage him/her to switch with the bass player every now and then to mix it up. By all means, have the audio and visual people cross train each other, as well as band members. By teaching each other, your group will stay continually challenged and perhaps find a refreshed passion for the worship experiences you all provide.

11. Inertia

The first year of creating contemporary worship is always the most difficult. It takes time to weather the pain of changing the culture at your church, to build up a new song catalog and to learn each other's musical languages. Once you do, it becomes easier. There are always growing pains, but hold on—you will get into rhythm eventually. In time, your focus can move from these growing pains to exploring new musical and liturgical ideas. As a ministry you will become strong but flexible. This process is like inertia. The momentum you experience after having contemporary worship for a while allows you to grow and feel a little more comfortable. With enough inertia behind you, it is possible for your ministry to survive without you.

A good measure of how you are doing as a worship leader after your first year is to assess how or whether the ministry will continue if you leave. If the answer is that it would fold up without you, emphasis needs to be spent on training others and creating transferable systems so your successors can be successful. You want to build a program, not just a band. If your ministry is turnkey, then you are doing it right. If you are experiencing hard times as you start a new contemporary service, just know that the longer you do it, the more likely you are to develop inertia. You will arrive! Hang on!

Section 12

Musical Diversity

1. Diversity in Song Leadership

2. Avoid Monochromatic Worship

3. Core Band

4. Other Instruments

5. Appropriate Instrumentation

6. Intergenerational Worship Teams

7. Guest Musicians

8. Children's Choirs

9. Band Exchange

1. Diversity in Song Leadership

Variety is the spice of life. Normally if you were to go see a band at a music venue, you would expect there to be just one lead singer. You probably also expect that this singer would lead most if not all of the songs. This is how commercial bands function, with the exception of bands like Styx, Fleetwood Mac, Caedmon's Call, all of which suffered from identity crises and eventually broke up.

In worship, however, there is significant value in having different voices lead your songs. Remember that excellence is your goal, not perfection. So if you have different lead singers within your group, try to spread around song leadership, even if it means that your very best singer does not sing all of your songs. It should go without saying that if someone does not have an adequate ability to sing, song leadership should not be imposed on that person for the sake of diversity. But when you do have multiple lead singers who are capable, mixing it up adds vibrance to your worship.

Building a system of diversity creates an open door for lead singers who want to participate on a limited basis. You may have in your congregation people who are great singers but don't have the time to practice or participate every week. Bringing them in to lead a song or two gives them an opportunity to share their gifts, adding richness and texture to the worship you provide without committing your guest lead singers beyond their availability.

2. Avoid Monochromatic Worship

The term monochromatic is one I use to describe a lack of diversity in sound and experience during worship. The word "bland" seems insufficient and perhaps too critical. When we say something is bland, we're saying we don't like it, that it is boring. Something can be spicy; however, if all you get is the same spiciness over and over again, it becomes boring and predictable, yet not bland.

This is why I like the word monochromatic, because it illustrates the lack of depth and vibrance that is otherwise available when we use a fuller spectrum. The adjective describes worship without much diversity in song selection, voices, instrumentation and styles. When all of our songs sound the same, led by the same voices, using the same instrumentation, we risk boring our congregations and ourselves.

Don't be afraid to venture beyond your group's sound. The songs that break the mold are usually the ones that get the strongest feedback. I think it's necessary to emphasize the profound importance of playing songs you as a group enjoy playing. If your band is tired of playing the same songs in the same way, it will show. The only thing worse than your band looking bored with a song is them trying to fake their enthusiasm about it. Mix it up. Keep it interesting. Find what works and trust that God's grace has brought you there and will sustain you. More importantly, trust in the grace of your congregation. They are hungry for diversity as well.

As I study contemporary worship services, the ones that strive to be different from other churches and strive to have different voices and radical song selections always fair far better in terms of growth and energy.

3. Core Band

In contemporary worship, it is possible to develop or settle into having a core band. There are advantages and disadvantages to this approach. One advantage of having a core band is that over time you will develop a sound and style that is your signature way of playing. In one of the bands I was in, the songs we played had a common sound to them. By playing together for as long as we did, we developed body language that helped us communicate timing, rhythm and direction within a song. As a group we became tight — an adjective of high praise among musicians.

With a core band, the congregation can also get accustomed to how you play. They come to worship with some expectation as to what they will experience. The predictability of a core band can be comforting to some congregants.

There are serious disadvantages of having just a core band, however. If every week you have the same four to six people offering music, it can become somewhat routine. Predictability, although comforting to some, is far less engaging to others and can lead to some musical boredom.

The major disadvantage of limiting your contemporary worship team to a core band is that fewer people have the opportunity to share their gifts through your ministry. The more people there are to share in the ministry, the more people will be engaged in worship. When you limit yourself to a core band, you lose many of the contours and expressions that bring vibrance and interest to your work as a musical ministry.

Ideally, you will find a group of musicians who function as a group, with an extensive list of guest musicians as well as alternate players. It may take longer, but over time you will develop tightness without sacrificing musical diversity.

4. Other instruments

This is an incredibly rich opportunity for a band. As a worship director, I've used banjos, mandolins, penny-whistles, accordions, cellos, violins, upright basses, steel guitars, Native American wind instruments, flutes, clarinets, saxophones, tubas, French horns, trombones, trumpets, harmonicas, turntables and all sorts of percussion. All of these wonderful instruments have enhanced the music we've provided. Being open to incorporate all of these different instrumental sounds allows us to incorporate a vast number of people who would not be able to engage in contemporary music so actively. Incorporating auxiliary instruments develops musical and intergenerational diversity by inviting musicians of all ages.

In my experience, I've used a large wind section to add some punch to songs on major liturgical Sundays. I've replaced electric bass with cellos to add to the emotion on certain songs. I've had accordion players instead of keyboards, which creates an earthy, more approachable sound on contemplative pieces. We've used xylophones and ukuleles to add a quirky, yet approachable sound to some songs. And I've used steel guitars to make some of our songs sound more like country music. These auxiliary instruments add color, warmth, depth and emotion to our songs and keep our congregations interested.

As a worship leader, especially one who's responsible for a band, I would encourage you to abandon any notion as to instruments that are off limits. As I'm writing this book, it does seem there is a big push towards a more acoustic sound in worship. The acoustic sound is somewhat reflective of popular music but is much more likely a push back from the electric sound that became prevalent in churches in the early 2000s. If you have someone who can play accordion, for example, an instrument that was considered the pinnacle of not cool not too long ago, you may find it can be incredibly effective coupled with an acoustic guitar and a cello and perhaps a cajon. Seriously, no instrument should be ruled out without consideration.

Once there was a song we were performing that had a ska style. Our percussionist really wanted to play a police whistle during parts of the song. I laughed and said to him "absolutely not!" He responded, "Yeah, I'm going to try it anyway" (exposing just how powerless I really was) and when he did, he was right. It really did work for that one song. I learned to be flexible, I learned to listen a little more and allow myself to be surprised.

5. Appropriate Instrumentation

Inasmuch as I would encourage trying different instruments, I would say it is very easy to overcomplicate a song by force fitting instruments into a piece where they don't belong. Early in my experience of worship leadership we had a flautist who played on just about every piece. Perhaps we were afraid of hurting this person's feelings, but some songs just don't benefit from a flute. As a worship leader, you will sometimes have to make decisions based on a profile of "less is more."

How many instruments (and voices) you have going at the same time on your songs can be affected by your worship space. In wide-open spaces with booming acoustics, you will especially want to avoid over complicating your music. If your music resounds and almost echoes, too many instruments at once will get messy. When this is the case, we can take a page out of the stadium-rock playbook. With stadium rock, instrumentation is limited, harmonies are a little less complex, drumbeats are not sophisticated. The ultimate stadium rock song is "We Will Rock You" by Queen. That song has a clear and defined lead vocal, limited instrumentation and an easy-to-follow signature beat. That's why it sounds so great in a huge echoing stadium. If you have a big booming acoustic space without a sophisticated system for managing it, just remember that less is more.

One last note on instrumentation: this is my own personal preference, but we should limit our use of tambourines. Call it a pet peeve, but it seems that tambourines are used in order to give somebody something to do. Let your percussionists make a decision as to whether tambourines add to or detract from what they're doing. As a student of contemporary worship and an attendee of a multitude of different contemporary worship services, I've seen the tambourine used in excess way too often. Use sparingly.

6. Intergenerational Worship Teams

The best churches are intergenerational. Younger folks bring vitality to the congregation. When young people are invested in congregational life, we all feel better about the future of our church. Having younger people involved in your congregation brings a vibrancy to all you do. Likewise, having mature members actively involved in your congregation brings wisdom, experience and a different, but just as important, vibrancy to congregational life. Churches that have a good balance between younger and older participants tend to thrive in worship, community service and congregational care — and they grow.[52] The benefits of intergenerational contact should be self-evident, but I think it's important to emphasize this powerful opportunity every congregation would benefit from developing.

Without a continuous effort to avoid it, congregations can become mono-generational. Denominational churches are particularly susceptible to this. Trends show that younger folks are leaving their denominational upbringing. Many of them are choosing to join nondenominational churches, while others still are choosing to settle in as part of the "church alumni."[53] Major denominational churches risk losing participation from younger congregants by not appealing to, or more importantly, not adapting to their worship needs. In contrast, new upstart, hipster, nondenominational churches are proving they can appeal to younger folks, but quite often risk a lack of intergenerational contact by not actively appealing to or welcoming older congregants. Neither situation is ideal and both require strategy for improvement.

With contemporary worship, we have a terrific opportunity to help foster intergenerational contact within our churches, starting with the worship leadership team. Think of your team as a cross section of the demographic you are hoping to have in your congregation. Try to have people from different generations in your band and AV team. If your band is comprised completely of people in their fifties and up, there's little chance that younger members are going to feel the same connection as they would if there were some younger members in the band. It works the same in the other direction as well. If your band is made up only of youth, it may be difficult for older members to have the same level of connection with the band and the music offered. Either way, having multiple generations represented in your band is a way to increase your band's relevance to your congregation as a whole.

In denominational settings, contemporary worship is viewed to be in competition with traditional worship. Having some older members in the band will help mitigate the inevitable marginalization that comes from some traditional oriented members who may consider contemporary worship a "youth thing." Likewise, having some young members in your group versus having all older folks gives you something different from what is typically offered through traditional worship and some pathways to connection with younger members. In summary, if your band is primarily made up of older folks, seek some younger participants. If your band is made up primarily of younger folks, recruit some older members.

I've found that by crossing the lines between traditional and contemporary worship, you can become more intergenerational as a church. Try inviting traditional worshippers to lead solos or play instrumentals in your contemporary worship on occasion. Likewise, try sending some of your contemporary musicians to lead a song in traditional worship every now and then. Also, see about coordinating combined worship services that use contemporary instrumentation and voicing along with choirs and pipe organs. The result is a more unified church, representing several generations.

7. Guest Musicians

Having guest musicians, be it from your own congregation or outside of it, can add interest, perspective and energy to our week-to-week worship. Constantly recruiting within your congregation is an important part of being a worship leader. You have somewhat of a captive audience when recruiting within your own congregation. Keep a list of people who want to share their musical gifts or any other creative talents. Keep that list at hand when you are planning your worship and always challenge yourself to find ways to incorporate these people into your program.

Finding guest musicians from outside of your congregation is another way to diversify your music. Inviting musicians from other churches is one possibility. An idea to pursue along these lines is to develop a network of local contemporary worship leaders. Perhaps you could form a group that regularly meets for breakfast, lunch or in the evening to discuss new creative ideas for worship. With such a collective, all the members of the group can vicariously contribute to other congregations by offering feedback and input. A wealth of knowledge is available when worship leaders gather together and talk about what works and what doesn't work for them. Through such a group, you may be able to set up a musician exchange program. It is also possible to use a group like this to organize band swaps. The possibilities for adding diversity to your worship events abound through active participation in a group such as this.

Incorporating guest artists can be a lot of work. Bringing in guest artists can also be risky in that you may not be completely sure of their ability or their message. Before inviting a guest artist, it's a good practice to vet them as best you can. By listening to online resources—or better still—hearing them live, you can have a good idea of what they may add to your worship.

I would suggest taking some time to talk with potential guest artists, perhaps over coffee or some sort of intentional meeting before deciding to add them to the worship. These meetings will be a good opportunity to make sure the message of the music they offer will be consistent with the stated beliefs of your church. In these brief meetings, talk about what songs may work well. Most cities have a number of professional grade musicians from which to recruit. Finding them may be as easy as posting something on a bulletin board at coffee shops and music stores.

Keep an ear to the ground for touring musicians traveling through your town. A simple phone call or email to an artist's agent takes very little effort, and they will most likely appreciate your inquiry. When contacting touring musicians, have in mind what you'd be willing to pay these folks, if anything. And be prepared for them to say no. Depending on the size of your church, touring musicians may see a benefit in having an area to sell merchandise after helping lead worship. You may be surprised at the willingness of some musicians (as I have been) to want to come and play.

Many musicians who travel really miss Sunday morning worship. If they are giving concerts on Friday and Saturday evenings, they are likely to be available on Sunday mornings. Remember that it doesn't hurt to ask; in fact most musicians will be flattered. Having knowledge of upcoming events, monitoring concert calendars and making phone calls are all part of getting this process started. Most touring musicians, Christian or otherwise, have at least one charity they are interested in supporting. A way to compensate these professional artists for lending their talents for your worship services is to offer an opportunity to promote their favorite charity. Remember that your worship space is a potential venue. Depending upon the size of your worship space, it may serve as a very attractive vantage point for artists who are looking to serve God through advocacy of a particular charity.

8. Children's Choirs

When selecting songs for worship, be sure to create spots for your children's choirs. If you don't have a children's choir, perhaps you can start a conversation in your church about creating one. If you have a children's choir, do what you can to get them involved with contemporary worship.

When you schedule your children's choir, you create moments that are more engaging for the young kids involved, as well as the parents and caregivers for those kids. I'll admit it seems silly to tout the importance of having a children's choir, assuming that this is obvious. But I am aware of contemporary services that never have their children's choir offer songs, and I feel strongly they are missing out.

Learning to sing in children's choir helps youngsters feel more comfortable with singing in church in general. As time goes on, many of these children's choir members gravitate towards being part of your traditional choirs or your contemporary worship team. Sowing these seeds is one way to help ensure the vitality of your worship ministries as the years move on.

In my experience, children love being around guitars, drums and other instruments. If you are able to provide a background band for your children's choir, they will be excited.

As a worship planner, try to schedule songs led by your children's choir at least once a quarter. Use your musical offering spots for these songs. Avoid scheduling the children's choir during gathering music, which may not be fully attended.

Likewise, avoid scheduling children's choirs to lead songs while the congregation is standing. You will want to give the congregation the opportunity to see and hear the children. The best way to do his is to have them sing while everyone is seated and listening.

Finally, schedule children's choirs with plenty of advance notice. It takes time for them to prepare a song, so give them as much notice as you can by including them in your seasonal planning.

9. Band Exchange

Another idea for adding diversity to worship is a band swap. Hopefully you will develop relationships with other worship teams in your area and can work out a Sunday where you switch places with the other team. It will be good for your team to get out of the building every now then.

Often your team will become more galvanized as you become ambassadors of your home church. Your congregation will be blessed by hearing some different styles. To really mix it up, develop relationships with praise teams that are considerably different from yours. For example, if your praise and worship team provides mainly acoustic guitar-driven rock songs, see if you can work out a switch with a gospel group. Hopefully, both congregations will be blessed by the diversity in style that the band switch brings.

Section 13

Music and Message

1. Choreography of Efforts with Pastors

Musicians understand the importance of harmony and rhythm. When we choreograph our songs with sermons and liturgy, there is a harmony to it. When we are deliberate about matching songs to sermons and liturgies, these elements stay in tune with each other and keep the same beat. When sermons, liturgies and music are all saying the same things in different ways, our worship services become powerfully instructive, edifying and soul stirring for ourselves and our congregations.

I would go so far to call it mission critical that the songs we play in worship reflect the theme of that day. Working in a choreographed effort with the Scripture, liturgy and message, songs can drive home a point. This requires planning and a diverse catalog of songs from which to choose. Coordination between message and music requires several meetings. For most pastors, their messages aren't finished until they're given on Sunday. It may be too much to ask to have sermons planned out months at a time, but it is possible to have some idea as to where the sermon may go, based on the scheduled Scripture.

If your church uses the lectionary, you at least have a starting point. If pastors, ministers, or whoever is giving the message can provide a few sentences describing where they may go with the message on a given Sunday, you will have something to work with as a song planner. It probably goes without saying that coordinating music takes a lot of time. As much as it is unreasonable to ask for complete descriptions of sermons months before they're given, it's equally unreasonable to expect a band to provide a complete set of on-message songs on a moment's notice.

If you're starting a contemporary worship service, factor in time for regular meetings with music staff and pastors. Being on the same page will allow you to be in sync and provide the most effective worship possible. A quick note for the pastors who are reading this book: if the music is already planned for a particular week, consider the lyrics of those songs as you write your messages. This may help you in your process while placing you on the same page as the musical message. Also, try to echo some of the lyrics from the songs in the prayers you lead. This builds synergy between song and message, allowing them to spill into each other.

When I meet with worship leaders, surprisingly many are unaware of just how powerful worship can be when the songs, Scripture and message are all saying the same thing. I will ask them about the criteria they use for choosing songs. In some cases, they pick songs based on what they think the congregation wants to hear. I've challenged these worship leaders, and I will challenge any readers of this book to use a different criteria for choosing songs. Our congregations expect us to lead. When we choose songs based on what we think the congregation wants to hear, we are essentially letting the congregation lead worship. This may be OK, but it will be just OK. If you endeavor to be an extraordinary leader, however, focus more on what your congregation needs to hear. Challenge yourselves and challenge your congregations by using music that can't be heard at any church on any given Sunday. Be different. Claim your voice as you choose your songs based on the message and Scripture of the day.

2. Music in Sermons

Sometimes music not only works in conjunction with the sermons; sometimes music can actually be the sermon. Music in sermons can help drive home certain points. As worship leaders, we continually strive to grab as much of the attention our congregations can muster. Sometimes it's necessary to mix it up in our sermons in order to keep people's interest.

Adding music to a sermon can be a catalyst for several congregants to pay more attention. A healthy dialogue between worship leaders and preachers will help facilitate this strategy. One formula for integration of music with the sermon could be to start the sermon off with a song the message is based on. Another format would be to close the sermon with the song, which punctuates the message.

Personally, I like when a song is used in the middle of the sermon where there's a set up, then a song, and then a discussion about how the message and song meet up. We are all finding that congregations have an ever-shortening attention span for sermons. Adding music within the sermons as a way to keep attention can be refreshing.

3. Know Your Theology

Decide what theological precepts are consistent with your church's stated beliefs. Theology should be an undercurrent to all of our worship planning. Denominational churches will have some clarity on their theology. The songs we choose to sing should be reflective of the spirit of our church's agreed-upon theology. Our songs need to be theologically congruent with our sermons. This mean we need to be theologically critical of the songs we choose. A mistake many of us make is thinking that if a song is good enough for the radio (K-Love, for example), it is good enough for worship.

When I was first starting out as a contemporary worship musician, I found out the hard way that this is not true. Once our pastor gave a 20-minute sermon that described how Jesus' time on the cross was carried out, not to make us feel guilty but to make us connect with the human Jesus. The message went on to say that the point of the cross was to give us an example of how love works, not punishment. The message concluded that the cross is an example of love and connectedness with God and humanity and not just bitter retribution. That Sunday our music director scheduled a popular praise song titled "Here I Am to Worship," which has the refrain "I'll never know just what it cost to see my sin upon the cross." There was a significant conflict between message and music here. Instead of compounding this thoughtful message with equally thoughtful lyrics, our song created confusion and worked against the hard work our pastor invested in his message.

Sermons and songs just have to be on the same theological page. Song lyrics stay with us differently than sermons. Lyrics are more likely to be recorded into our long-term memory. When lyrics are inconsistent with sermons, they undo the teaching our pastors work to convey. We should all remember that our songs teach, and we should avoid teaching anything we will have to later un-learn. Taking a few minutes each week to check in with pastors to review song selections could be very helpful.

Knowing your church's theological stances helps to both broaden and narrow your song choices. For example, your congregation may be very serious about the first commandment "Put no gods before me." And your congregation may interpret that to mean that no other religion other than Christianity has divine value. If that is your congregation's stated beliefs, it would not make sense to play Bob Marley's "One Love." If your congregation has made the theological decision that we can learn from other religions, however, and that all people are treasured and celebrated creations of God, then perhaps that song would be welcome and celebrated.

Here's another example: Your congregation may have a very strong stance against homosexuality. If that is the case, you may choose to not incorporate songs written by and composed by openly gay people. Or, perhaps your congregation believes that God is big enough to love us all and create us all and has a much more progressive opinion on homosexuality. If the latter is the case, prominent gay songwriters like Jennifer Knapp, the Indigo Girls, Elton John and others are available for your catalog. Knowing what you believe helps you sing more emphatically and serves to pull music and message together in a choreographed effort.

Do you need a Masters of Divinity in order to be a worship leader? No, but it helps. It may not be practical for all worship leaders to have advanced degrees in religion or theology. It does, however, benefit any worship leader to have some theological understanding.

I would not suggest rushing out and trying to read and digest all of Paul Tillich's *Systematic Theology*, but I would talk with clergy about some theological resources that may be a little bit more accessible. Popular theologians like Marcus Borg, John Dominic Crossan, and Barbara Brown Taylor do well in writing theology for laypeople. Emergent writers like Shane Claiborne or Brian McLaren should be required reading if your church has adopted a more progressive theology. Personally, I think Rob Bell's writing is excellent. He tends to be more controversial, and he is not given much street-cred in academic circles, but his clarity and vision is contagiously compelling and richly informative for worship leaders.

Part of taking the role of worship leader seriously is accepting the mandate to constantly improve. The more you can learn about theology, the smarter you will be about your song choices. Being grounded in theology helps you to appreciate lyrics more. It will help you jettison lyrics that are inconsistent with the adopted theologies of your particular church. If you're able to dig deeper into the more sophisticated world of theology and start reading Neihbur, Tillich, Barth, Moltman, Zinsendorf, and a holy host of others, your understanding of Scripture will take flight.

I would suggest beginning with the theological writings that are foundational in your denomination. Lutherans read Luther. Presbyterians read Calvin and/or Zwingli. Methodists read Wesley; Catholics read Aquinas, and so on. Whatever your faith tradition, learn your history and the thinking of its framers so when you choose songs, you can engage their lyrics on a deeper, more personal, more intellectual and more liturgical level.

Section 14

Song Planning

1. Plan a Season at a Time

2. F.U.S.s Principle

3. Listening versus Singing

4. Share Song Selection Process

5. Length of Songs

6. Pay Attention to How Songs End

1. Plan a Season at a Time

A primary job function of a worship director is choosing songs. There are several variables to consider when picking the ideal songs to match your Scripture and themes. This task is not to be taken lightly or done at the last minute. The calling to lead worship is a gift. To be good stewards of this gift, we must invest time and effort into the process of selecting songs for worship.

I've found that seasonal planning works best for worship planners who are striving for artistic diversity and overall excellence. There are several advantages of planning a season at a time: First, it allows you to plan out your new music. When you look at the entire season, you can take a list of new songs you would like to incorporate, and then place them according to the weeks where the Scripture and hopefully the sermon theme will fit. This allows you to appropriately manage your band's efforts. More importantly, with enough up-front time, you can send out lyrics, lead sheets, sheet music and links to new songs so the band can work on their own to prepare for these new pieces.

Second, those in charge of preparing bulletins and multimedia will benefit from the advance notice. Respecting the time of the people who handle the administrative functions surrounding contemporary worship, such as projecting lyrics, preparing bulletins, and sound engineering is responsible and forthright. Respect honors their contributions.

Third, planning a season at a time allows for scheduling of special guests. Guests can be instrumentalists, vocalists, special liturgists, or perhaps liturgical dancers. All of these folks, usually volunteers, need time to prepare whatever it is they will be offering. If you don't know what you're playing until that week, it's very difficult for additional people to be prepared.

For example, let's say you want to have liturgical dancers for one of the songs you'll be preparing. If you tell them on Tuesday what the song will be and expect them to be ready by Sunday, that's quite a bit of choreography that has to be hammered out in an unrealistic time frame. Instead, if you plan a season at a time, you can let participants know when the song is scheduled so that they can have multiple practices on their own, as well as with the band to make sure timing and execution are done correctly. Likewise, guest soloists and instrumentalists are more likely to be available and be better prepared with advanced notice.

Fourth, when planning music, looking at an entire season at a time allows you to make the best placement of certain songs. There may be a song that does just a serviceable job one week, and then the next week is perfectly on theme. If you are managing your worship plans from week to week, it's possible you may use a song one week that would really work better in one of the following weeks. Planning a season at a time allows you to make the best calendar placements of songs within your available catalog.

Fifth, planning a season ahead of time allows you to post your future song lists so everyone in the group can know what's coming up. More importantly, soloists will know when they will be leading songs. This is particularly helpful with scheduling. For example, it's been my practice to post all of the song lists for a season at a time in our band room. This provides band members a central location to view what songs are coming up, what sheet music to pull for practice, and/or Sunday worship, and also functions as a central calendar for planning time off. Of course the seasonal worship plans are sent electronically as well so all concerned can have quick, mobile access.

For most churches I've worked with, the seasons are as follows: 1. Holidays: Thanksgiving through Epiphany, 2. Pre-Lent: that strange time in January and February, 3. Lent: Ash Wednesday through Easter, 4. Spring: Easter through the end of the school year, 5. Summer: at the end of the local school year through the beginning of the school year, 6. Fall: beginning of the school year through Thanksgiving. I've found that this breakdown works well for organizing our calendars.

I recognize that for many of us it is difficult to free up several hours in a row to work on seasonal planning. I would strongly urge us, however, to consider the likelihood that it will take far less time to plan seven or eight weeks in one session than it does to plan seven or eight weeks in seven or eight different sessions. Planning worship a season at a time gives you an extraordinary amount of control over your worship services. When we wait until the week before to plan our worship, the tail wags the dog and you can only hope to be as effective as seasonal planning by accident. Being a leader means having a plan, a vision and a strategy. Seasonal planning helps you do your best, to be the most effective as you live out the work you are called to do.

2. F.U.S.s Principle

In contemporary worship, there should be a mixture of songs that are considered musical offerings and other songs the entire congregation feels comfortable singing. Musical offerings may invite the congregation to listen more than to participate, and that is okay. You wouldn't want to make an entire worship service out of musical offerings, however.

Likewise, it is possible to make all your songs in your worship service congregational, and there may be some folks who would prefer it that way. I think, however, that a worship service functions best when there's a mixture of congregational songs as well as musical offerings. For songs that are congregational (i.e. opening and closing songs or anytime the congregation is invited to stand and sing), there are some guidelines for choosing songs. I suggest using the "F.U.S.s. Principle." The F.U.S.s. principle is an acronym I made up when we were starting to renovate contemporary worship at First Lutheran in Greensboro, NC. The acronym stands for F – Familiar, U – Upbeat, S – singable, and the extra S stands for "silly."

Let's start with "F"— Familiar. When the congregation is invited to sing along, it helps that the song be familiar. Older hymns come pre-loaded with this familiarity and make for good selections as your opening and sending songs. When you want to add new songs as opening and sending songs, you will need to build congregational familiarity with the piece, both with lyrics and melody. You can come at this in several ways. By using your musical offerings and gathering music to introduce new songs, you can gradually build familiarity until the congregation is comfortable enough to sing along with it as a congregational song. Also, it's a great idea to teach the chorus of a new song to the congregation before playing it for the first time. Using simple instrumentation and one voice leading the melody, you can invite the congregation to sing along with you as an introduction to the song.

Congregational participation in worship is vital and should be nurtured. The more familiar the congregation becomes with the songs you offer, the more likely it is to get fuller participation. The downside of familiarity is that the songs can become predictable and even boring. If your band is tired of playing a particular song, there's a good chance the congregation is growing weary of that piece as well. To address this, be deliberate about how you use your gathering music and your musical offerings to constantly expand and refresh your catalog of familiar congregational songs.

Songs with simple, repeating choruses (i.e. songs from Chris Tomlin, Hillsong) tend to be immediately familiar. Be very judicious with these songs, however. Many songs that come from the praise and worship genre tend to run on and on and can get a little tedious. A brief survey of the negative response against contemporary worship reveals there is an animosity building toward songs that are too repetitive, claiming they build a false sense of emotion. These songs are very familiar and singable, but they are growing increasingly less useful in worship.

The "U" stands for upbeat. I've been in debates over whether congregational songs have to be upbeat or not. I've concluded that the congregation is best served by using upbeat songs as sending or closing songs. There are some exceptions to this axiom. For example: on a Good Friday service, we thought ending with a more solemn song seemed to capture the mood better. This is the exception, however. Usually you're going to want to end with the song that is upbeat. Similarly, your opening songs are opportunities to build energy in your worship service. Unlike songs at the end of your service, your opening songs can set the table for whatever your theme is for that day. That being the case, if your theme is solemn and reflective, your opening song could be the same. The sending song, however, is most likely the song that the congregation sings in the parking lot and on the way home. Keeping the sending song upbeat starts your congregation's week off with a spring in their step.

"S" stands for singable. When the congregation is standing, you want them to sing along. Offering songs that are singable means making some tough choices. You may have in your group a brilliant soprano or tenor who can blow the roof off the place with stratospheric high notes, but you also realize their voices are tough to follow. When making sure your songs are singable, you have to consider the key in which the songs are written and what the highest notes are. Typically, you don't have to worry as much about the notes being too low (think of George Beverly Shea), but if the notes are so high that the congregation can't sing along without switching to falsetto, experiment with the key to see if you can fit it better with the singers in your congregation.

Songs become easier to sing when they are led by multiple voices. And when I say multiple voices, I mean multiple voices singing different octaves of the same melody. Now, I love harmony. The congregation also loves harmony. But when we want a singable song, the harmony should only accent the melody and not be heard above it. Your sound techs can be very useful in making sure the melody is dominant.

Finally, if the song is too wordy, it may be difficult for your congregation to sing along. For example, I use a number of songs from the Dave Matthews Band. Their songs can be tough for congregations to sing since they are often wordy with intricate rhythms in the verses, thus relegating the songs to musical offerings and gathering songs. A good way to measure whether or not you have a singable song is to consider how long it took you as a group to figure out how to sing it. If it takes several hours for musicians to learn how to sing a song, it's unlikely that song will be suitable for your congregation to sing.

Applying the F.U.S.s. principle to your opening and sending songs will optimize congregational participation. Use this idea to guide not only the songs you choose but how and when you play them.

3. Listening versus Singing

My guess is that just about any focus group on contemporary worship in any church anywhere in the country will conclude that they want to be able to sing more. They want every song to be singable by the entire congregation. I am sure, however, this is not what is best for effective worship. Certainly, contemporary worship should provide ample opportunities for congregants to sing, but I have found that offering opportunities for the congregation to just listen is equally effective and equally appreciated. Musical offerings that engage the Scripture and message can work wonders for conveying meaning and driving home the points of the day. Ideally, there should be a mixture of songs that all can sing and some when all listen.

The balance of these types of songs is a matter of taste. A good rule to follow is this: if the congregation is standing, play songs that are easy to sing. Incorporate at least one song that the congregation has the option of just listening to. I understand people want to sing. My assumption is the same compulsion that leads church members to want to sing during worship also compels them to be more vocal in their opinions about worship. Their voice is not the only voice in your congregation. By offering songs your congregation can just listen to, you are representing a silent majority of people who want to take the time during musical offerings to listen and reflect on the message. Men especially appreciate the opportunity to just listen to songs in worship. The people who don't necessarily want to sing every song are not going to tell you. Instead, they will thank you for songs that allow them to just listen.

4. Share in Song Selection Process

One of the best ways to move your musical group to buy into the mission and objectives of your music ministry is to invite them into the worship planning process. Seeking the band's input can be done in several ways. You can simply ask for song ideas while you're together at practice or you can send an email to everyone and ask for their feedback. The most effective way I've found is to have what I call "listening parties." At listening parties, we gather together and listen to the new song ideas we may have as a group. One idea is to use a large easel with dates and one sentence themes for each of the weeks we are trying to program. As you and your group listen to new song ideas, ask "Is this a song we want to do?" And if the answer is yes, then ask, "Does this fit any of our upcoming themes?" Other questions should be raised as well: "Does this song translate well to live performance?" "How much time and effort will it take to prepare a song with a complicated arrangement?" "How do we do this song our own way?"

Once you settle on a list of potential musical offerings, then plug those songs into the most appropriate weeks based on their theme. If there are new song ideas you cannot fit into upcoming weeks, add them to your song ideas list to be reviewed next time you have a planning session. Then, encourage your group to work on filling in the rest of the song lists for the upcoming weeks. This process can be time intensive, but it pays to get your team more invested in planning. Having your team involved in the planning process does slow it down, but it adds diversity, creativity, as well as overall investment from your volunteers in music ministry.

5. Length of Songs

As we choose songs to fit certain time frames, we should consider how much time a song takes. A common practice in nondenominational contemporary worship settings is to take a song with a worshipful chorus and draw it out, offering worshipers a chance to lose themselves in the ecstasy of the song. I've seen worship teams take a song that's normally 3-1/2 minutes and draw it out to over 10 minutes. I have not, however, seen this practice in denominational settings, and I certainly wouldn't recommend it. Overextended songs can be off-putting to some worshipers (myself included). One of my mentors called this style the "24/7" approach — singing the same 7 words, at least 24 times. I have shared healthy dialogue on this subject with some of my nondenominational friends. They explained they try to create moments that allow the Holy Spirit to work through their congregation. For them, they deliberately draw these songs out until they're moved by the Holy Spirit to disengage. Their congregations are just into it.

For most denominations, however, this style of worship leadership doesn't fit into our more rigid worship time frames. I would never discourage anyone from creating moments in worship dedicated to the invitation of the Holy Spirit moving us and working through us. In denominational worship, however, for the most part, we have an obligation to stick to our worship plans so that other elements in worship (sermons, sacraments, and prayers) also have the time and attention they deserve.

On a personal note, I think the invitation of the Holy Spirit to work through our songs can happen just as well in 3-1/2 minutes as in 10 minutes. The length of our songs doesn't and shouldn't have any bearing on whether or not the Holy Spirit is more or less present. Over-extending songs has far more potential to turn off and turn away participants than it does to engage them. If you finish a song and the congregation is left wanting more of that song, that's a good thing!

6. Pay Attention to How Songs End

When picking songs, attention should be paid to questions like: What does this song leave the congregation with? What feelings will people take away from this song? What is the lasting impression of the song? The way we do the outros on our songs can affect the answers to these questions.

For example, if you want the song to capture the desperation or angst found in many of the Psalms, try an unresolved ending. Or, if you want the congregation to be celebrating with joy at the end of the song, finish the outro with a big, unison hit. If you want to transition into another liturgical element, just dial back the intensity and instrumentation of the song to function as a background for the next thing (prayers, communion verba).

You can even change the way a song ends in order to convey meaning. For example, the song "Oh Come, Oh Come Emmanuel" is usually played in E minor. By changing just the last chord in the song to E major, it communicates a sense of hope at the end of the song. Minor chords communicate a more dire feeling, while major chords are much more upbeat. Music can tell a story of hopeful waiting in ways that words, gestures and inflections alone are limited in their portrayal.

Jeremy Begbie suggests that in modern Christian worship "delayed gratification" is rarely reflected in our music. He suggests that music can be a powerful tool to facilitate learning on prayerful patience and hopeful anticipation.[54] Unresolved endings can help facilitate this feeling. As you select songs, remember that you can adjust the way a song ends as an effort to fine tune a song selection within your worship plans.

Section 15

New Music

1. Develop a Deep and Wide Catalog

2. Church Music

3. Find New Music and Stay Ahead of the Game

4. Traditional Hymns

5. Recordings versus Live

6. Speed and Tolerance for Learning New Music

7. Send Links

8. Original Songs

9. Songwriting

10. Changing Lyrics

1. Develop a Deep and Wide Catalog

In order to have songs available to fit specific themes throughout the year, it's necessary to have a broad catalog of songs from which to choose. I've held conversations with worship leaders who disagree that a deep and wide catalog of songs is necessary for worship leadership. They argue that you should work to perfect about thirty songs, spending your energies on getting those songs tight. I think this is a good strategy if you are a touring band, offering the same set at different venues each week. But repeating the same songs over and over again will eventually bore your congregation, as well as your band mates. More importantly, the breadth of potential scriptural topics cannot be adequately covered by thirty songs.

If your church uses the lectionary, in the course of three years you will experience 156 different scriptural themes. It is our job as worship leaders to engage that Scripture and do our best to tell those stories through music. A broad catalog of songs to choose from helps tremendously toward that end. Contemporary worship allows for a vast expansion of the songbooks we use. Original songs are more easily procured, and songs that would not be included in most hymnals are now available. Contemporary worship more readily allows us to look beyond music that would be marketed as Christian music as we build a more diverse catalog from which to choose.

2. Church Music

The categories of church music are a moving target. I'm not going to try to distinguish between praise and worship versus contemporary Christian since there is a preponderance of resources that try to make these distinctions.

For me it's easier to qualify church music as any music that reflects Scripture and the mission of the church. This is a broad brush stroke. There is just so much music that can be used to tell God's story. I think orchestral pieces can vividly describe God's majesty. I've used jazz pieces to retell the story of creation. Heavy rock songs can powerfully capture the emotions that lead us toward seeking salvation. I think hip-hop songs can bring God's joy into perspective and reflect the struggle against oppression. I think bluegrass songs can draw out the sadness of Good Friday and celebrate the joy of discovering the Resurrection. I think reggae songs invite us to share in Jesus's vision for global unity. And I think classic hymns connect us to our rich Christian traditions All this music is church music. I would never suggest limiting ourselves to songs that are classified by record companies as praise and worship or contemporary Christian.

As Christians, Jesus is our leader and our example. Jesus was often found where religious people would not expect him to be. As worship planners, we should look for Jesus in unexpected places as well. When we earnestly search for Jesus, we find Him. When we look for songs outside the prescribed categories we are given, I believe God honors that quest and delivers to us a diverse, expressive, effective and vibrant musical catalog.

3. Find New Music and Stay Ahead of the Game

As a contemporary music planner, you should keep an ear to the ground for new music that will help tell God's story. Many of us who lead contemporary worship in a denominational setting rely on contemporary Christian radio to supply us with ideas for new songs. Because so many churches do this, it is difficult to claim much originality for your service if you're pulling from the same extremely limited list as everyone else.

Let me recommend instead that you search for new music by using online music streaming resources. Challenge yourself to listen to music you would not otherwise hear. To accomplish this, refrain from using stations with generic all-encompassing titles like Christian Rock or Contemporary Christian. Instead, find music you like, create a station for that group and see what comes up.

Most of these online resources have the ability to bookmark songs you can go back to and review later. Here's an example of how that worked for me: I enjoy the music of the Avett Brothers, so I created a station for them. After listening to that station for a while, the song "Starlight" by the Wailin'

Jennys came on. I was mesmerized by that song. It does a wonderful job of retelling the story of Jesus on the cross. It's an aggressive song with banjos, complex harmonies and intricate timings, but I knew we had to play it. So we worked on the song and had it ready to play for Good Friday. Afterward the feedback from our congregation was exceptional.

From there, I researched the band and found a song called "One Voice," which is a simple, yet profoundly beautiful song we wound up playing in both our contemporary and our traditional services as a means of building our collective community. Both of these songs blessed the congregation, and I would have never discovered them without online music services. One of my fears is that I will eventually lose my ear for contemporary music. Listening to online music streaming services helps keep me aware of new music, styles and trends.

Since time is always limited, explore ways to do music research while accomplishing other tasks. Try listening to new music while you are cooking or cleaning. If you commute, listen to new music while you are traveling. (Please don't try to bookmark songs while driving!) My advice is to never settle for what they give you as far as your song catalog is concerned. Be curious and pray as you seek new music. Be original and make your group's catalog your own.

Also, if the area you live in has a live music scene, it's a great idea to get out and listen to live music. Staying in tune with indie music is a good way of staying ahead of what will become mainstream. If you can go to several smaller venues with unsigned bands, you can get a feel for what is likely coming next. Most importantly, it's fun! It's fun to go listen to music. Enjoy yourself, get lost in it, and embrace your passion for music by listening to others perform. And don't be shy about wearing earplugs if it gets too loud!

By staying ahead of music trends, you can work to avoid the correct criticism that contemporary Christian music tries to copy popular music. For example: around 2007-2008, it became quite hip to use banjos. Bands like Mumford and Sons or the Decemberists found success and momentum in their new-folk style. Fast forward to 2013, and you see bands like

the Rend Collective Experiment and even Casting Crowns doing second-hand copies of this style, several years behind the
trend. For this reason, I love bands like Jars of Clay and Gun-
gor. These groups, who are unapologetically Christian, don't
sound like other bands. They always work to carve their own
path. They stayed true to their Christian message while gaining massive appreciation from a variety of listeners and critics.
Be timeless. Be a vanguard. Be the church that others copy.

4. Traditional Hymns

When choosing songs for contemporary worship, don't
rule out or forget about hymns. We know that hymns are most
often sung by a choir and accompanied with an organ or piano.
During a typical traditional worship service, there may be four
or five hymns that don't change much in their arrangement
and instrumentation. It is easy to lose or miss the complex melodies and rich lyrics found in many traditional hymns as they
get washed in the routine of well-rutted instrumentation and
choral arrangement.

Taking classic hymns and adding new instrumentation
and new harmonies does well to bring out the song's original
beauty. I find myself falling in love again with songs that I sang
my whole life by listening to them in different arrangements.
Experiment with this; take familiar hymns and try out simple
acoustic versions. Add violins, mandolins, cellos or accordions
and see how these melodies can be revitalized.

One year, St. Patrick's Day happened to fall on a Sunday.
That morning we offered "Be Thou My Vision," a beautiful
traditional Irish hymn. For arrangement, we used an acoustic
guitar, a mandolin, an upright bass, a bodhran (a traditional
Irish drum) and a penny whistle for the interludes. The sound
was very Irish. We added a liturgical dancer who is skilled in
traditional Irish dance. Together we offered something that
celebrated Irish heritages, and we gave this traditional hymn a
new purpose in a dynamic way.

I couldn't imagine a modern song that would be as moving. Since hymns are usually familiar to your congregations,
go ahead and use them as opening or sending songs, or any

time the congregation is invited to stand and sing. Find ways to do classic hymns your own way.

5. Recordings versus Live

As we choose songs for worship, it is tempting to just use a track for accompaniment on a new piece. I see this frequently used for children's choirs, which is OK. But, when adults sing along with tracks, it has a real karaoke feel to it and is useful only in the event that live instrumentation is absolutely not achievable. I found that an acoustic guitar can be extremely versatile and that stripped-down versions of songs with live accompaniment are far more effective than singing along to a track. It is more work, but I would encourage you to pursue due diligence on finding a way to provide live accompaniment whenever possible. Tracks, because of their predictability, may prove a bit more useful for liturgical dance, but beyond that they should be used sparingly or not at all.

6. Speed and Tolerance for Learning New Music

What is your group's speed and tolerance for learning new music? Each group will need to assess their speed at learning new songs. As a worship leader, I've always been blessed with talented people who can learn songs quickly. Still, I found that it was stressful on our group, as well as our congregation, to introduce more than one new song a week. We have gone beyond one on some occasions, but we knew it was not a sustainable pace.

It's a good idea to have periods of time when there are no new songs, when you can refresh, reinvent and improve on songs you already know. The groups I have led use the summertime when several people in our group are on vacation, as are many members of the congregation, to take a break from learning new music so we can work on our existing song catalog.

A terrific idea for working on new songs, if you can pull it off, is to take a one-day or two-day retreat with an emphasis on learning new music as a group. This strategy can cover so much ground very quickly but is, of course, dependent on the availability of your group. Doing this will give you a jump-start if you are just starting out, or a kick start if your band is in a rut.

In my tenure as a worship leader, I have held an event like this only once, so I recognize that this idea, despite its considerable merit, is logistically difficult to pull off. Talk with your team, explore possibilities for retreats, or perhaps just a Saturday when you can focus on new music. Consistently adding new songs will keep your band and your congregation invigorated. Having these new songs at the ready allows you to confidently schedule them for upcoming worship themes.

7. Send Links

In earlier days of contemporary worship leadership, we had to create CDs to hand out to individual members of our music group so that we could all get an idea of what a song sounds like before we started learning it as a group. Thankfully, those days are over. Sending links to songs is much faster and more convenient. When you come up with your worship plans, hopefully way ahead of time, include links for any new songs your group will be learning. Don't forget to send these links to the audiovisual team as well so they have an idea of the song's timing for lyrics projection. This will allow your team time to become familiar with the song beforehand.

Some members of your group may want to create their own lead sheets. Sending links gives them an opportunity to listen and come up with lead sheets that are written in a way that works for them. Many of the songs will not have sheet music available. Even if the sheet music is available, it's rarely exhaustive of all the instruction needed for a particular piece. Sending links helps fill the gaps and function as a guide as we work through our lead sheets and/or sheet music.

Finally, post links for upcoming songs to your church website. This allows congregants an opportunity to become familiar with upcoming songs, enabling them to better sing along when the time comes. Sending links to all interested parties ahead of introducing new songs helps speed up the process and allows you to move more quickly as you expand your musical catalog.

8. Original Songs

Contemporary worship offers considerable flexibility for utilizing original songs. Most contemporary worship leaders who I know are also singer/songwriters. Some songwriters map out every note of their original songs, but the predominant paradigm for originals in contemporary worship comes from a simpler approach. Most of us write out lyrics and chords, leaving time signatures, harmony lines, bass clefs, and the like to the interpretation, skill and creativity of our band members. This simpler approach lends itself to faster turnout from the point when a song is just an idea to the point when that song is offered in worship.

Original songs can be written to meet a particular theme. It's been my history to write songs when there's a theme for which I don't have a specific song. For example, after the tragedy on 9/11, I wrote a song called "From the Ashes" as a means of engaging the topic and offering my church community an opportunity to collectively mourn and heal. I was able to write the song in a day and have the arrangement worked out within a week, which allowed us to offer the song into worship at the peak of its relevance.

Using original songs also allows songwriters within your congregation an opportunity to participate even though they are not necessarily part of the band. There may be folks in your congregation who are not musicians but are skilled poets who may be able to lend their literary gifts toward the creation of a new song. Original songs help define your music ministry and should be firmly supported. Congregations, in my experience, respond well to the time and artistry given to writing original music. There is something special about the only church offering your original song is yours. It helps build a unique identity for your worship community.

Remember that with originals, it is possible to have too many. I would suggest not having more than one original in any one worship service. There may be exceptions here, but the assumption is your originals will be less familiar to the congregation, which may hinder their ability to participate in the song. So use originals, but spread them out.

9. Songwriting

Songwriting is not for everyone. Skillful songwriters are somewhat rare. If you have someone in your group who can write effective songs, certainly nurture that gift and provide space and opportunity for it. Songwriting workshops or classes can certainly help in developing this skill. Contemporary worship leaders are sometimes presented original songs from the group that are, frankly, not very good. As a worship leader, you are placed in a precarious position. The best way to manage original songwriting within your group is to ask to be involved in the creation of the songs.

What you want to avoid is having someone spend hours and hours writing a song, and then present it to your group in a mostly-completed state. That leaves you and your group little room for adjustment to the song without potentially hurting the feelings of the songwriter. Let your group know that when they write songs, you would like to receive rough drafts while they're working on it. Try to avoid taking over the creative process, but do invite yourself to be in a position of first right of refusal.

When writing original songs, there are no rules, but there are some guidelines. Amateur songwriters commonly write songs without good structure. They frequently include too many bridges, fail to set distinct choruses and lose symmetry in their verses. They may need help organizing their work so their songs don't become run-on sentences, but instead have form and function. Make sure any original song actually conveys a message that is consistent with the mission of your ministry.

On several occasions, members of my band and from our congregation at large have submitted original songs to me with the hope of incorporating them into worship. I was able to accommodate some of these songs. But more often than I would've liked, the songs submitted to me were preachy, guilt-oriented and in one case, just mean. For those songs I had to tell the writers "thank you, but no." (The toughest job a contemporary worship director has is saying "no.")

When listening to original music from members of your team, keep an open mind, an affirming voice, and tactfully offer advice for making the song better if needed. Songwriters' songs are their babies. It's easy for a songwriter to take it personally when you want to make edits. Working with them before the song is complete will help mitigate the potential for hurt feelings. But if the song is not going to work, be strong, stand your ground, and do what's right for your ministry by saying no. When the songs are good and consistent with your mission, originals can be a powerful form of expression. They significantly build the body of work that your group produces. They can help make your group unique and provide diversity and flexibility to your musical catalog.

10. Changing Lyrics

Contemporary worship leaders can further expand the catalog of songs to choose from by changing lyrics to songs that would otherwise not fit their worship settings. I mentioned earlier that by not using hymnals, contemporary worship allows for a great deal of flexibility in changing lyrics. I have on several occasions changed lyrics to guide songs toward specific themes and to avoid outdated theology.

I don't take the decision to change lyrics lightly; I take time to deliberate before choosing to alter another artist's work. I've encountered varied opinions on this idea as I talk to contemporary worship leaders. Many of us who are songwriters appreciate the original integrity of the lyrics chosen for songs and resist changing lyrics altogether. Making this decision should always consider and weigh the intentions of the original writers.

For example, we had a theme that John Lennon's song "Imagine" would fit very well. We talked about changing the lyric "Imagine there's no heaven" to something more theologically sound for Christians, but we couldn't get around the fact that Lennon, a genius songwriter as well as a secular humanist, included that line as part of the structural integrity of the song. Most of us musicians decided that we would rather not do the song than try to change it. Then, to our surprise and edification, on New Year's Eve 2012, CeeLo Green sang "Imagine" in Times Square, choosing to change the same lyric. The public was outraged, and we felt justified in our decision.

Changing lyrics is usually as risky as the song is familiar. If a song is too popular and the lyrical changes are extensive, the song is no longer a cover, but a parody. This is not a completely bad thing. Parodies can be very fun and useful. (I mentioned earlier how we wrote a parody of the song "Our House" by Madness for a building campaign, which we performed with a full wind section in all of its Ska-glory to rave reviews.) For the most part, however, if a song you are making lyrical adjustments to takes on more of a parody form, it's best to rethink using it unless the intention is to be a parody.

Section 16

Considerations When Choosing Songs

1. Music Can Help Congregations Overcome

2. Healing Through Music

3. Worship as a Way of Life

1. Music Can Help Congregations Overcome

When selecting songs for worship, we should remember that music can provide our congregations with an outlet for crying out when we are suffering. Music can unite us as we collectively express and share our struggles. The Psalms were songs written to glorify God and empower us to claim hope for justice. African spirituals were sung in defiance of the system of oppression that surrounded those who were enslaved.

Music can unify congregations and embolden them to take action. Music can inspire the masses and at the same time meet individuals in their personal struggles. Music can help people be resilient. I've come to discover that the paradox of powerlessness is resilience. When songs reflect divine justice, when they reflect the upside down, overcoming, revolutionary, radical message of the Gospel, they provide a means for people to mitigate their fear and anger over oppression and injustice. These songs inspire us to hope and nurture our ability to carry on, building our resilience. Songs that sing of hope and trust in divine justice serve as a means to collectively share the struggles of life as a community. These songs serve as a means of coping with life's pains and as a means to celebrate victory over them.

2. Healing through Music

Margaret Kornfeld in her book *Cultivating Wholeness* writes about how worship can have a powerful impact on a congregation's well-being or "wholeness."[55] She asserts that sermons, songs and liturgies can be structured and guided toward preparing a congregation for inevitable hardships and can profoundly affect the healing process for members who have experienced loss. Few of us (none of us) will go through life without experiencing trauma, grief, depression or profound loss.

When we worship leaders choose songs, we have an opportunity to provide healing events for our congregants. When we choose songs without much substance that just play on disingenuous emotion (as is the case with a good number of the songs in the praise and worship genre unfortunately), we miss the opportunity to create a healing space for worshippers who are going through trials in life.

Songs that deal honestly with hurt, pain, fear and doubt do a marvelous job of connecting people who are hurting with the reality that they are not alone. Honest songs give people space to hurt and question. Honest songs help us as worship leaders to share the journey of healing with our congregations. For example, the song "Your Hands" by JJ Heller does a simple yet powerful job of telling the story of someone with unanswered prayers who musters faith to go on. We've performed that song several times at Sunday worship as well as at funerals, and the response from the congregation has been extraordinary.

Using songs that authentically meet people where they are does much to help people cope and to work towards healing, finding faith in the darker times. Faith can be a struggle at times, especially when we are hurting or ashamed. Songs like "Doubting Thomas" by Nickel Creek do well to remind our congregations that even doubt is covered by grace.

Most pastors know the power of the pulpit for affecting change in the lives of congregants. Sermons can equip us for life's challenges and can empower us to face the hardships that we all must inevitably face. The songs we provide in worship have a similar potential, if not a greater one. Choosing songs that help mitigate grief, loss, depression and anxiety can do wonders for members of your congregation who are hurting.

Inasmuch as music can cultivate wholeness, it can also deepen hurt and shame. Songs that are too preachy or that inspire guilt should be removed from your catalog. I would encourage you to spend time thinking about your lyrics and how someone who is hurting might receive them. Have discussions with your pastors to decide if a particular song sends the right message and achieves the goal of serving your church's pastoral care objectives.

3. Worship as a Way of Life

When we plan worship, we hopefully will choose songs that people can take with them throughout the week. How much joy it brings me to hear people in the parking lot singing one of the songs we offered in worship! Use songs that function as ear worms, that guide our thinking toward the Gospel message. When we sing these songs to ourselves, our worship becomes portable, helping us to let worship become a way of life.

Section 17

Managing People and Processes

1. Excellence versus Perfection

The best thing I learned from Rory Noland's book *Heart of the Artist* was the difference between excellence and perfection.[56] As musicians and as worship planners, we often set perfection as our goal. Perfection is a lousy goal, however. It is unattainable, and it sets the table for disappointment. Excellence, on the other hand, is a terrific goal. Excellence as a goal leaves room for improvisation and forgives minor mistakes. Excellence reflects the character and the individual gifts of each band member. Perfection is rigid and exact. Perfection is closed ended. Excellence, however, is expressive and open-ended. Excellence as a goal provides freedom not only to make mistakes but to create something new, something beyond the original composition. Excellence is a lofty goal: it is dynamic, it is ever changing and adapts as the congregation evolves. As we endeavor to lead and manage music ministries, celebrate the excellence in what we do, and avoid the inevitable frustration from seeking perfection.

As worship leaders, we hope to honor God with our work. We are to do our best with what we have with a humble and hopefully joyful spirit. Expecting perfection of ourselves is neither humble nor joyful. Perfection as a goal is prideful, and it can make us miserable. When we combine our time, talents and our joy together, we create something better than just perfectly executed musical notes. When we set excellence as our goal, we honor God by acknowledging that we all fall short of perfection, and it is only through God's ultimate grace and goodness that we or anything we create can be perfected.

2. Prayer Time as a Group

Time is the currency that a worship leader has to spend. A worship leader's responsibility centers heavily on managing how a group spends its collective time together. Worship leaders invest time in learning new pieces and getting the music tight. Contemporary worship leaders rarely have enough time. When we try to manage all of our volunteers' schedules, time becomes a very scarce, precious resource. It is almost counter-intuitive to stop making music to deliberately check in with each other as a small group, to review prayer concerns and praise reports, to talk about the meaning of your music and to just be prayerful. But as impractical as it may seem, taking time to check in and pray together is an essential use of your team's time and energy.

As a worship leader, you have an opportunity to take the reins as a small group facilitator. I would suggest looking at your music ministry as a prayer group who comes together and makes music as a result of that prayer. I found making time to pray together to be vital in preparing us and sustaining us as a group. If you feel you don't have time for checking in and praying as a group, consider cutting something else.

Prayer time together should be a priority for a team that hopes to effectively share the Gospel. If leading group prayer time is not something with which you're comfortable, bring in someone who has skill facilitating small groups. Every practice session should incorporate some form of group prayer.

To begin prayer time, you may want to either gather the group together in a circle or sit somewhere facing each other and begin with some simple questions. I normally ask if there are any praise reports or prayer concerns, and then I look around waiting for responses. Once we've talked about our prayer concerns and praise reports, we conclude with prayer. As the director, it's a good idea to not be the one doing all the talking, so if you have folks in your group who are comfortable leading prayer, invite them to lead your closing prayer.

Whether we pray at the beginning or the end of practice, group prayer connects us to our shared goal of spreading the Good News. Finally, group prayer is necessary to begin any worship service. Praying together centers us and works to remind us of the importance of our mission as musicians. It builds our focus and places our devotion to God at the forefront of all that we do.

3. In the Band versus Being Part of the Congregation
Microphones, guitars, keyboards, drums, and all create literal and metaphorical barriers between worship leaders and the rest of the congregation. Being in the band can easily sepa-

rate you from the congregational worship experience. In some ways, you are detached from everyone else.

Addressing this can be challenging. Depending on how many people you have available as musicians, one effective way of breaking down these barriers is to have some of your musicians sit out for a song or two and sing with the congregation. Another way to move past these barriers is to step out in front of the microphones, lay down the instruments and lead the congregation with just voices. Whether we are talking about contemporary bands or traditional choirs, there is still a disconnect between those leading the songs and those following along. By removing the physical barriers of microphones and instruments on occasion, it's easier to embrace the oneness of your congregation.

One of my favorite bands is known for singing three-part harmony. Towards the end of their show, the three of them stepped in front of their microphones to sing an a cappella piece. It was easily my favorite part of their performance because I felt more of a connection with them and had a much more tangible sense of their presence. If your band is not currently offering any a cappella pieces, I strongly encourage you to consider adding them.

One group I spoke to about this said, "We're a rock band, we don't do a cappella." I explained to them that because they are a rock band, it is that much cooler if they can do a cappella! I pointed out to them that Queen, arguably one of the greatest rock bands of all time, is known for complex harmonies and skillful a cappella pieces. As I urged them to consider an occasional a cappella song, I reminded them that the best strategy for minimizing the disconnect between your music group and the rest of the congregation is to occasionally get physically closer and move past physical barriers like music stands and microphones.

Besides physical barriers, praise teams risk being separated from the rest of the congregation, establishing social barriers. It is best if the members of your worship team travel in many different social circles within the congregation. It is easy for your team to become its own clique, creating an us/them image with the rest of the congregation. Encourage your team to explore and try out different Sunday school classes, different service functions and different committees if possible.

4. Volunteers — Communications

When managing volunteers, you'll need to develop a communication strategy that best fits the people with whom you're working. If you have a diverse musical group, you will need a diverse communication strategy. Sometimes over-communication is necessary. If there's an important item needing to be sent out to everyone, sending a text, an e-mail, posting a note at church, and making phone calls may all be necessary to get through to everyone.

Communication is key. Finding a common resource, particularly a common calendar is essential. I used to write on a paper calendar and that worked well, but once everyone started using smart phones, I began sending worship calendars electronically. For me, the calendar includes our weekly song lists with instrumental and vocal assignments written out. By marking on that calendar the Sundays band members will be absent, it helps us all plan better to accommodate their absence.

If you're blessed enough to have multiple people for the individual roles in your band or group, having an accessible calendar really helps. There are software programs that help with band management. I've experimented with these and found their potential effectiveness by far exceeds their actual, practical effectiveness. I am cautious about using any software that has to purchased, installed and maintained by each member of the group in order to communicate. Instead, I prefer methods that are accessible and functional with software already resident on everyone's phones or computers.

5. Expected and Unexpected Absences

Recruit, recruit, recruit! Never stop recruiting. Hopefully you'll have in place a system that schedules your musicians months in advance. In a perfect world you will know when someone will be out and can schedule a backup or modify your set to accommodate their absence. Sometimes, however, things come up and you have to make adjustments on the fly. Having a roster of backups is extremely useful here. If you use different people for the same role, you can protect yourself against being shorthanded. Having multiple people in the same role provides diversity, and it protects you from having to do without important personnel on short notice. Likewise, it is good to have a list and a budget for musicians who can be called in a pinch. Having musicians for hire available on short notice makes for a reassuring cushion when the unexpected occurs.

Depending on where you are in the country, inclement weather can also play a significant role in your planning. Be mindful of your volunteers by writing out and distributing your inclement weather policy well before it's needed. With backups, alternates, emergency substitutes and contingency plans in place, you can feel more confident as a leader that you are doing your part by being prepared.

6. Affirmation

As a worship leader, it's your job to remind your team about the importance of the body of work you all are putting together. You normally are the primary recipient of positive feedback from the congregation. Be sure to share that feedback with your teammates. Remind them of the value and importance of their efforts. As you and your team collaborate to create effective worship experiences, be aware and share the good news that your collective work is part of something that will touch lives and be part of the foundation many people build on in their own walks of faith.

Your worship team is a small group. Making time for small group check-in and prayer is essential to building your team and staying connected to the mission to which God has called you all. During this time, it's a great idea to offer affirmations to the members of your group. As artists, we know it takes dozens of affirmations to make up for one criticism. Using this time to build the group, to remind them of your mission and how you're completing it is essential in building a group identity. This can do wonders for developing long-term commitment to your group. When your team looks and celebrates their body of work, it builds a sense of purpose and identity.

During your group time, typically after practice, you may be able to do some intentional team-building activities. My favorite activity is one that seems a little corny, but it is powerfully effective in developing group harmony and affirmation. It's called "Names in a hat." For this exercise, write everyone's name on a piece of paper, fold them up and place them in a hat. Have each member select a random name, and then have them say two positive things about the person whose name they drew. The exercise is finished when all the names have been selected. What results is a deliberate time of group affirmation that builds up our confidence, our worth, our self-esteem and equips us to be graceful as we receive grace. Again, I know it may be a little uncomfortable, but I've never heard of anyone regretting doing this exercise. On the contrary, I've had a wealth of positive feedback from facilitating this game.

As a worship leader, you have an opportunity to care for each of your team members' sense of worth as it pertains to your worship. Musicians place themselves in a very vulnerable space. We are easily hurt, and if we suspect that our artistry is not appreciated, it can affect our performance during worship. Genuine, honest affirmations inspire us and keep us focused and motivated on our mission to offer excellent worship experiences.

7. Making the Most of Our "—"

My former pastor offered a sermon titled "Making the Most of Your Dash." In the sermon he said that all of us live our lives between two numbers. The first number is the year we were born and the other number is the year we die. In between those numbers there is a dash "—". In this sermon he talked about making the most of that dash, because it is all we have.

That message had a profound impact on me and helped me realize there is a finite amount of time to accomplish the things I want to accomplish in life. Moreover, it encouraged me to celebrate the body of work I have already developed, and it invigorated my desire to do more.

In music ministry, each week we add to a body of work we're creating. Every worship service is part of a collection, whether we record our services or not. The worship events we create exist in the minds, hearts and souls in our congregations. They exist in our memories; they become our traditions and build our legacies, which exist well beyond our dashes. Celebrate the body of work you create as a worship leader. Remind your team of the importance of this work and how they are using their "—" to create something beautiful, something that lasts. Remind them that when archaeologists dig up things from past generations, the items they become most excited about is the art. Remind yourself and your group that you are artists, you are creating new traditions and leaving a heritage for those who will follow you.

The person who taught me how to be a contemporary worship leader, whose job I eventually took over when she retired, was a visionary, an organizer, and an artist. When she announced her retirement, I wanted to give her a gift that was personal and meaningful. Using Photoshop, I created a 48" x 48" framed poster. The poster had in its background several different square and rectangular images, making it look very much like a quilt. Within each of these squares and rectangles, I placed the titles of all 767 different songs she implemented during her time as contemporary worship director. She was deeply touched by this gift. This gift allowed her to hold in her hands symbolically the body of work she helped bring about. This framed poster is one of her most prized possessions. She displays it proudly, and she even painted her living room to match the colors found in the poster.

The work we do is important. Celebrate it! Be proud and make the most of it.

8. Vulnerability and Criticism

Playing music places us in a very vulnerable space. Always be aware of the vulnerability we experience when we put ourselves out there by playing music. As a leader, recognize that you are in an even more vulnerable position when leading several musicians. If you find yourself dreading practice or carrying a tremendous amount of tension when dealing with musicians or the congregation at large, it helps to recognize your own vulnerabilities. Acknowledge that affirmations help mitigate the anxiety associated with this vulnerability. Likewise, we should recognize this vulnerability predisposes our sensitivity to criticism.

It seems like a healthy band should be able to offer constructive criticism in ways helpful in improving the overall quality of the work they do. The vision for constructive criticism is a careful and caring imposition of advice directed toward altering a person's way of doing something. In a perfect world, this criticism will be presented to a person, and that person will respond positively and be thankful for the constructive advice. Now let's get back to reality. There is no such thing as constructive criticism. In fact, I would urge you as a worship leader to remove the word criticism from your leadership vocabulary. Criticism always hurts. Criticism usually deconstructs. When our art is criticized, we either take it personally or ignore it. I recommend replacing the word criticism with two other words: coaching and collaboration.

Coaching and collaboration are terms that better accomplish what we intend to do with constructive criticism. I recommend these two words because of the power dynamics involved with constructive feedback. If you are the leader of a group and you want to help develop one of your team members, the feedback you're giving them about the behaviors you want them to change is not criticism, but coaching. As a leader, you should be empowered and feel the responsibility to help others to continually become better at what they do as members of your team. A healthy relationship between a worship director and a team member implies that the worship leader will provide guidance as you collectively work toward excellence. Coaching is expected and appreciated.

As members of your team help each other to become better at providing quality worship, it's important they have the freedom to collaborate and work out a collective agreement as to what works best. Allowing team members to criticize each other is a recipe for dysfunction. You, as a coach, can inspire your team to collaborate instead of criticizing. When team members collaborate, it balances power dynamics, unlike criticism, which places some members of the team above others. The term collaboration implies that members of the team are looking to be collectively better, where criticism implies that someone is wrong. When we collaborate, we ask questions. When we criticize, we give demands. Collaboration is dialectic. Criticism is didactic.

9. Check Your Motivations

In music ministry, you will have people who want to volunteer for the wrong reasons. In my conversations with worship leaders, it seems everyone has stories of people who insist on getting airtime so that the congregation can be blessed by their talents. I have several stories of people who have nagged and complained about not being given ample opportunity to sing solos, despite the reality that they are not outstanding singers. Performing in church is a rush; there is immediate gratification that comes from offering music, which can be very edifying. This cannot be our motivation if we want authentic, relevant worship.

In the event someone is not motivated by sharing the Gospel but wants to use your music ministry as a stage to show off, I found you can quickly defuse the situation with a few targeted theological questions. By asking, "What does this song mean to you?" or "What is God saying through this song?" you can get a conversation going so that the song becomes more important than the person offering it. Once you've established that the message is more important than the messenger, you can help them see why you choose or don't choose to have them lead the song. If you do have them lead a song, this process will help ground them in the song's meaning and purpose.

It is just as important that we, as worship directors, make sure we are not motivated by accolades from performance but are fed instead by knowing that God has made some use of us through worship ministry.

10. True Ownership

As contemporary worship leaders we simply must share the spotlight. Musicians, or creative people in general, can be insufferably territorial. We claim ownership of creative material and are often deeply offended at the suggestion we relinquish any claims to our creative works. In contemporary worship, if someone usually leads a song vocally, it becomes their song. We do the same thing with instrumental roles, styles and arrangements.

When we are asked to step aside to let someone else do what we normally do, it is easy for us to be hurt, to feel as if we were not good enough, or feel displaced. While it is always important to celebrate the gifts of your team and to acknowledge the excellence each team member brings, it is equally important to work towards musical diversity. Worship leaders do well to develop a culture of generous collaboration. By saying things like "We don't own any of this" or "It is wonderful to share this ministry," we set into motion a fundamental understanding about how the work we do is bigger than ourselves or our individual abilities.

As a worship leader, it's important you lead the way on allowing other people to handle vocal and instrumental leadership, even if you have always been the vocal or instrumental leader. By setting this example, it will be easier to ask your group to share the responsibilities they would otherwise lock away to themselves. Be reminded that the surest sign of ownership of something is the ability to give it away.

Here's an example: Perhaps you have someone who does a terrific job leading a particular song vocally. As you recruit among your church's youth for musicians who want to share their talents, you find a youngster who wants to sing that particular song. Your usual soloist for this song may be hurt by being asked to give up the solo role on this piece, so you tactfully ask that he or she share this ministry. Remind the soloist that true ownership is demonstrated by giving something away. Ask if they would not only support this decision but help this youngster in preparing to lead the song. In tactfully engaging the situation, acknowledging the potential for hurt feelings, and being proactive about how to handle it, you can go from a potentially painful situation to one where a collaborative relationship is formed.

In summary, creative people are territorial. It's good to recognize this and challenge this, placing the focus on the mission of your ministry. Sharing the Good News requires that we share our ministry.

Section 18

Conflict Management

1. Conflict: Not Necessarily a Bad Thing

2. Systems Dynamics – Triangles

3. Different Musical Languages

1. Conflict: Not Necessarily a Bad Thing

Margaret Kornfeld's book *Cultivating Holiness* does a great job in explaining how conflict within a congregation can be healthy or at least a sign of healthiness. With musicians and visual artists, you likely will be dealing with people who are passionate and expressive. As artists, we care about what we do, we invest a large part of ourselves emotionally into our work, and we're usually protective of our vision. Managing creative people has its headaches. But just like any relationship, some conflict can be a sign of health and not necessarily a harbinger of doom.

Conflict can be a result of dysfunction, of course, but it can also be indicative of collaboration. So don't fear conflict. Instead, manage it as a tool for growth. When disagreements arise, first establish that the disagreement is over music and not over personal traits. Keep the conflict on task. If group members are in sharp disagreement and are not being tactful in asserting their opinions but are attacking other members personally, most certainly it's time to intervene. You want conflict in your group to be an exchange of ideas, not an exchange of blows.

Although you want to be collaborative, as the leader of your worship team it is necessary that you don't let conflict get out of control. Allow everyone to have a voice and seek out compromise in order to produce your best effort as a worship team. As a leader, if you find yourself as one of the combatants in conflict, always remember to keep a cool head and center on the love you have for this ministry. If disagreements are beyond navigation, it may be best to change the subject and schedule time to talk individually with the persons involved. On occasion, some outside arbitration may be necessary.

As a last resort, invite the senior pastor or someone else who is seen as an authority figure in your church to weigh in on your disagreement. I will warn you not to be optimistic about disagreements just going away. Again, artists are passionate people who believe in what they do and are willing to fight for their opinions.

When there is healthy conflict, it demonstrates that your group feels freedom to disagree. If there is no conflict at all, that means differing opinions are silenced or suppressed. Conflict shows that the individuals in your group are aware their voice is valued and are willing to use their voice to advocate their perspective.

When the conflict is just plainly unhealthy, you have options to consider. If the conflict that arises is among paid staff, you have considerable more leverage to insist they communicate in healthy ways. As for volunteers, the opportunity to participate in your ministry hopefully is an incentive they find valuable enough to want to communicate in healthy ways within your group.

If there is conflict that cannot be arbitrated, cannot be adjusted, cannot be worked through, and you've given it a fair opportunity to be resolved through all the means of your disposal, it may be necessary to ask a volunteer to stop participating. If you ever have to face this unfortunate circumstance, think of creative ways of redirecting the energies of this person. If it becomes clear that a person or group of people cannot function in a healthy way within your group and you come to the decision they need to be asked to resign, think about other ways they can use their skill and energy within the mission of the church.

Finally, if you have absolutely no conflict in your team, perhaps you are a tyrant. It's hard to imagine a group of creative people never having a disagreement. If that's the case, you may have developed or inherited a culture where it is not okay to voice an opinion, particularly one that disagrees with leadership. As a director you should always ask for feedback, always seek out creative input. Let your band know it's okay to disagree with you. They should know you may not act on every suggestion, but you will listen, discern, and seriously consider their feedback.

There is a terrific song by the band Switchfoot called "Love Alone is Worth the Fight." This song does a beautiful job of expressing that it is worth fighting for the love we have for God, music, and each other. The song does an equally good job of expressing how some of the other things we find ourselves in conflict over are just not worth it. I've used this song once in a quarrelsome meeting, and it helped us move past the conflict and on to the important business of music ministry.

2. Systems Dynamics – Triangles

As a worship leader, a rudimentary understanding of systems dynamics can be very helpful in avoiding unhealthy work relationships. A common form of systems dysfunction is known as triangles.[57] As Christians, we believe that when two or more are gathered in Christ's name, so too will Jesus be present. The joke in many churches, however, is "When two or more gathered, they're talking junk about someone else."

All too often, triangles form when someone has a disagreement with another person in your group, and they may attempt to enlist you to their side. This places you in a strange position. You want to listen and honor their concern, but you also don't want to form any sort of alliance that isolates or marginalizes other members of the group. One of the healthiest and most successful worship teams I'm aware of has a "no whispering" policy. Their strategy is to respect each member of the group enough to be direct with them and actively avoid talking behind each others' backs. This is a difficult task. But for the health and effectiveness of your worship team, adopt a policy that restricts any criticisms about other team members when team members are not present.

For example, let's say your piano player comes to you and says, "The bass player is always too loud, and I've heard complaints from the congregation about how loud she is. She's such a diva and probably needs her hearing checked."

Ideally, as a leader we might respond like this: "Thank you for bringing that to my attention. Let's have a discussion together about this at our next practice." What happened here is this: a member of the group tried to bring us into a triangle. Instead of forming the third side of this triangle, we rejected the invitation to gang up on the other member and moved the complaining party more toward open conversation.

3. Different Musical Languages

Some musicians use sheet music with full musical notation for learning and playing music. Others use lead sheets,
which are usually just lyrics and chords with minimal instruction. I've worked with people who have degrees in music who
need completely written out sheet music in order to feel comfortable with a piece. I've worked with several musicians who
cannot read sheet music and are only comfortable with lead
sheets. Working with both of these musical languages at the
same time can be a challenge. Each form has advantages and
limitations.

Lead sheets are the language of choice for most contemporary worship bands. They do not cost a lot of money like sheet
music does and can be created for any song. Since they are
rarely over three pages long, they fit on music stands and do
not require page turns. This is particularly important to guitar
players. Lead sheets can be used by musicians of varying skill.
Original music in contemporary worship is usually written
out in lead sheet form.

Lead sheets leave a lot to interpret. They require that you
have a good feel for a song before trying to play it. Lead sheets
usually have to be created, meaning they are a lot of work for
directors. They usually do not show time signatures, melody
lines, dynamics nor measure counts. There are plenty of internet resources for lead sheets, but they are never sufficient on
their own. Lead sheets have to be worked up and run through.
When creating lead sheets, I typically reserve about three hours
per song to hammer them out so that they are useful, clear
resources for the musicians in my group. By only providing
chords, lead sheets are a particular challenge to keyboard players who rely on sheet music for melody lines, leaving them to
either learn them by ear or to improvise on their own.

Sheet music or full musical notation does well to communicate the nuances of a song. It allows musicians with advanced skill to learn songs quickly and provides instruction on
more complex pieces, keeping members of your group literally
on the same page. Sheet music usually displays in detail the
melody lines for vocalists and instrumentalists. Sheet music

can help in discerning harmonies and can enable your group to pull off very complex, intricate pieces that would otherwise be impossible.

One disadvantage of sheet music is that it is very long. Piano players can spread written music out across the length of their keyboard, requiring fewer page turns. The rest of us use music stands. If you're a guitar player or a drummer, you'll need a music stand large enough to spread out the entire set of sheet music since you will not have a free hand to turn pages.

There are electronic resources for sheet music that run on tablets that do have timers in them to turn the pages electronically. At the time I'm writing this, tablets are becoming more popular, and one can envision a time in the near future where written music is managed electronically. I would look forward to that but for now tablets are expensive and impractical. The biggest problem with sheet music is that not every piece is available. This could seriously limit the catalog of songs you have to choose from. Finally, sheet music costs money. I normally spend around $5 per song, which adds up over time.

Leading contemporary worship music requires you not only be able to read sheet music, but you should be able to play with just lead sheets as well. Not every song is going to be written out with every note, every time signature, and every clef accounted for. It's important to respect the musical skill of the people who work with you, and it is a delicate balance to apply a tension that inspires these musicians to try new things. My best advice is to have fun and invite them to have fun with the music; then see what happens.

When I was first starting as a worship leader, I was working with our keyboard player, who was also our traditional music director for over twenty years. She was quite uncomfortable with lead sheets, which we were starting to use. She doubted her ability to improvise, using the lead sheets as a guide. I challenged her to just play. She did, and it was awesome! She came up with some bluesy funky piano runs that really added to the song we were working on. From there, she became more comfortable with lead sheets and found a renewed joy in just playing music.

Likewise, many musicians are unaccustomed to using sheet music and cannot function when the only music that's available are extensive musical notations. For these musicians, I think it's equally important a healthy tension be placed on them to learn how to interact with sheet music. Ideally you will have a mixture of musicians—some who use sheet music and some who do not, interacting and helping each other to develop their musical skills and talents.

Don't allow a pecking order to develop in your band over degrees of skill. Members of your group who do not read sheet music could easily feel lesser-than. Remind your group that we are all sharing our gifts and developing them in the process. Every member is important and needed. Someone may not have a lot of skill, but they have loads of talent—or loads of skill, with little talent.

A band working together to sharpen each other's talents and skills is a ministry unto itself that dynamically serves itself and the congregation. As a contemporary worship leader, you should challenge yourself to be able to function in both of these worlds and speak both of these languages. Being able to play music with just chords over words is important, and being able to read sheet music opens up a whole new world of possibilities, especially on piano-led pieces.

Not being able to speak the same language within a group can be a major source of tension. Musicians with advanced musical skill, perhaps even a degree in music, can become easily frustrated when the written music is not mapped out with the detail they are expecting. Likewise, musicians who do not use sheet music but use just lead sheets can be easily frustrated when musicians with different skill sets struggle to play naturally. If you experience this dichotomy in your group, be open about it. Talk about these differences. It's important to remember that one style is not better than the other. Reading sheet music is a skill, playing naturally is a talent. By having both of these musical languages working together, your group can develop its collective skill and talent and optimize its potential.

♪♪♩

Section 19

Dealing With Resistance

1. The Entertainment Argument

2. The "Performance" Critique

3. Applause

4. Male versus Female Vocal Leadership

5. Focus Groups

1. The Entertainment Argument

I've been leading contemporary worship most of my adult life. I've heard the critique: "We don't come to church to be entertained" more times than I would care to remember. I agree that our motivations to come to church and our experiences at church should be fixated on becoming mature followers of Jesus. But for worship to be meaningful, it must be carried out in ways with which people connect. Often persons who are threatened by contemporary worship confuse this connection with entertainment.

Describing the joy people experience in contemporary worship as mere entertainment is a deliberate attempt to marginalize and downplay contemporary worship as a legitimate alternative to traditional worship. If by being entertained we are offered meaningful representations of the Gospel that grab our attention and connect us to a deeper understanding of our faith, it is hard to argue it's a bad thing. Furthermore, the opposite of entertainment is boredom.

A rather uncreative response to the entertainment critique is to say "better entertained, then bored." I would venture much beyond that sentiment to say that entertainment is never our goal for worship but rather engagement and connection. Entertainment occupies our attention for a moment and then lets go.

In Christian worship, we seek to command the attention of worshippers and connect them to our religious message in order to learn and be equipped as followers of Jesus. Traditional worship accomplishes this for many of us, but for more and more of us contemporary worship does a significantly better job.

If you are confronted with the entertainment argument, take that opportunity to examine what it is you do. If you find that your motives are in order, don't expend mental energy trying to deal with this critique. Instead, invite whoever is offering this critique to make suggestions as to what they would change specifically. If they offer any suggestions, consider them and apply them if they help you accomplish your goals. If they don't have any specific suggestions, thank them for their feedback and feel free to move on.

Finally, it is good to remember that entertainment is not necessarily a bad thing. Movies like *Schindler's List* and *It's a Wonderful Life* are classified as entertainment, yet they carry profound messages. Television shows like "Little House on the Prairie" or "The Grinch Who Stole Christmas" are very entertaining while teaching valuable life lessons. Imagine if these movies and TV shows were shut down because they were too entertaining. Worship is art. And it's OK when art entertains us.

2. The "Performance" Critique

Similar to the entertainment critique, you may have congregants complain you are too "performance oriented." As I speak to worship leaders around the country, it seems we all share this struggle. Finding a balance between sharing your passion for music and not appearing as if you're giving a performance is tricky to maintain. As we use more sophisticated sound systems, different lighting techniques, and use spaces without natural light, we run the risk of looking like a show.

I don't disagree that contemporary worship can be performance oriented. I think those of us who lead worship should be aware that it is incredibly off-putting to some worshipers when they suspect your team has stopped leading worship and has started performing for performance sake. There are some practical ways to help avoid this. Let me start by saying I have yet to find a way to completely resolve this critique but the following has worked to minimize it:

First, get some natural light in your worship space if you can. Church experiences for most of us, if not all of us who grew up in the eighties or earlier, would include natural light of some sort. When the lights are all dimmed around us, we have less of a connection with the other congregants, bringing our focus to the stage. This may be acceptable if that focus were on the sacraments or on the sermon, but having that kind of attention placed on your worship team during music inspires the performance critique.

The challenge here is that most of us use multimedia to project our words on screens, and we are limited as to how much light we can bring into the room without obscuring the text on the screens. Take time to see how much light you could bring into the room during these times so that worshippers can see each other, bringing less emphasis on to your worship team. If natural light is not available or your worship is at night, explore ways to light the worship space so that people can see each other and your eyes are not compelled toward the stage alone.

Next, musicians should use very few spoken words. Leave the speaking roles to other people for the most part. Many of us as worship leaders, particularly those of us who are song leaders, are compelled to talk about a song before or after we play it. That may be necessary on occasion, but I would do this as sparingly as possible to avoid being too showy. As I mentioned earlier in this book: if you find you have to explain your songs too often, it's a safe assumption you need to pick different songs, ones whose meaning and relevance to the message are self-evident.

Finally, be real. Don't use overly dramatic gestures to get people to clap along or become over-emotional beyond what you are actually feeling. Often, the performance critique can be broken down to a feeling that the worship leaders are being disingenuous. If the music moves you, then move; if the lyrics break you, then break. If the beat makes you clap, then clap. But don't force any of these things. Be sure to center yourselves through prayer prior to leading worship. Invite God to work through you, make your music an offering to God and pray that the Gospel will be reflected through your ministry. Then just be your authentic selves as you perform for God's glory.

3. Applause

On the subject of applause during worship, let me start by referencing Psalm 100, which reminds us we are all entitled to, challenged to, invited to, and perhaps expected to make a joyful noise as we recognize the gift of God's grace. I personally don't have a problem with applause during worship and have yet to hear a satisfying argument as to why applause can somehow negate sacredness. My view on the subject is far from doctrine, however. Applause in worship can be downright startling to some people. Even though there is no scriptural basis to prohibit applause during worship, it is a prevailing culture in denominational churches to refrain from applause out of a sense of reverence. I think it's important to recognize both sides of the equation and make choices based on what is best for the people with whom you share congregational life.

A common argument against applause during worship is that it's a violation of the sanctity we ascribe to the symbols of sacrament. Applause seems too colloquial for those who would want to protect this sense of mystery and sacredness. Applause, for some, steals from them the opportunity to let silence do its job in helping a song sink into our minds and hearts. One argument I've heard several times against applause in worship is "We are here to praise God, not the band." These people concluded that when they offer applause, it is just for the worship team and not the worship event. For those I talk to who reject applause as a legitimate part of worship, what they feel is strong and they should be taken seriously.

As I mentioned, I support applause in worship. Applause is a joyful noise, and it allows a connection between the entire congregation and the worship team. There is a connection through applause that invites a deeper sense of community. Often, members of your worship teams include younger musicians. And, of course, when younger musicians are offering their talent, even the most traditional worshippers are inspired to offer applause.

I think it's possible to have applause in worship and not assume that the applause is for the band itself. Sometimes applause is a recognition of something good with which you have connected. Have you ever been to a movie that was so good that at the end the whole theater broke into applause? Who were we applauding? Were we giving praise to the film projector? Were we congratulating the movie theater for offering a great movie? Were we offering applause to all of the creative people who participated in making this film? My point is that applause sometimes is used to celebrate a moment and not necessarily particular people.

Here's another example: I used to go to dances when I was a kid. We would play songs on the stereo and then dance to those songs. At the end of each song, we would applaud. Who were we applauding? Were we applauding the stereo? We were applauding the moment. The point is this: applause can be very much the appropriate response to dances, good movies, or any event with which we find a connection and celebrate with others. Applause need not be a culmination of a performance, but a celebration of a meaningful moment we share together as a community.

So what do you do? How do you deal with applause? You could always take either one side of the equation or the other. If you are compelled by both sides of the debate, there is a third way. It is possible to manage the applause that happens during worship so that it is offered at the most appropriate moments and minimized during moments when it's less appropriate. This approach takes planning and choreography with the pastoral staff.

For example, if there were a song that you do not want to have applause to follow, have your pastor position herself or himself to begin talking immediately at the end of the song—preferably with arms raised to visibly get people's attention. This will expedite the transition into the next liturgical event without applause. If there are moments in your liturgy that are immediately preceded by songs and you want to avoid applause, try ending the songs differently than usual. Don't let the song end abruptly. Let it trail off by discontinuing the vocals at the end of the song but continue with instruments until your pastor has successfully transitioned into the next element. I found this technique to be particularly effective when prayers immediately follow a song. It takes some planning to do this seamlessly, but it makes for powerful moments in worship.

Let me conclude on the subject by noting that applause is a natural response I've seen develop among the congregations I have led over time. I have found that applause is something a congregation grows into; it's a sign of evolution. Applause can be considered a sign of growth and comfort within your congregation. I've been part of intentional efforts to completely suppress applause of worship, but I've never seen these efforts work. My experience tells me that congregations want to applaud. My advice is to be professional and strategic about applause. Manage it to your congregation's benefit. Don't try to stifle it; embrace it for its liturgical value.

4. Male versus Female Vocal Leadership

I hesitate to include anything about this topic since I don't want to add any legitimacy to this debate. This discussion carries with it a distinct sexism. If I am to attempt to write a comprehensive survey of the challenges contemporary worship leaders face, it makes sense that my personal experience with this dilemma be mentioned.

A while ago I was a volunteer on a worship team led primarily by women. These women had amazing voices. They were talented and skillful. They led most of our songs, and none of us on the worship team thought there was a problem. It turned out that a few members of our congregation contended they could not sing along to any of the songs the women led. They said they couldn't find their place in the melody. Both men and women complained, arguing that male voices are easier to sing along with for them.

As a result, the contemporary worship director assigned more solos to another male singer and to me. I didn't find out till later the reasons behind this, but when I did, I felt awful. My thinking on the subject was and is this: the congregation is best served by diversity in voices. It need not be all of any one thing. My experience tells me that congregations respond to and sing along with female-led songs just as much as they do male-led songs.

I do want to encourage as much participation as I can get out of the congregation. Therefore, it's always been my task to provide harmonies and octaves on songs so that there are different places for people to connect while singing. For example, if we are having a song that's led by a soprano, we will have

someone else take the octave below where that soprano is singing. The octave below is not necessarily the lead, but it provides a line for folks who have less stratospheric voices with
which to sing along. Choosing an appropriate key for your
songs is helpful as well. This strategy maybe is more work, but
I would throw away any notions that men or women are better
or worse at leading songs.

One final note: It is not a good use of our time to chase
down every complaint that comes through. This work requires
a thick skin and a steely resolve. When complaints come in that
lack specifics, challenge those persons complaining to move to
more manageable issues. In this case, the complaint was com-
municated as "we don't like women to lead songs in worship."
This complaint in this form is very hurtful and sexist. As I discovered later, I was friends with the people who levied this
complaint, and I knew they did not intend to be this offensive.
When we worked to clarify the complaint, we got to the real issue: these people wanted to be able to sing along but could not
sing with one particular person who used a wireless headset.
We made some simple adjustments in our sound system and
all was resolved. By moving on to the real issue, we were able
to implement strategies that addressed the actual issue.

5. Focus Groups

Sounds like a good idea right? Focus groups are formed
to provide input so that different perspectives can be represented. In worship ministry, it is vital that the needs of the congregation are being met and the idea of focus groups seems
to be a way of making sure the voice of your congregation is
represented in your ongoing worship planning.

The functional reality of focus groups is that they limit
artistic expression and diffuse creativity. Worship leadership
is an art form. If the Beatles had solicited and complied with
feedback from focus groups prior to making the White Album,
it would have never been made. Focus groups would advise
Jackson Pollack to paint less abstractly. Focus groups would
have advised Elvis to tone it down.

When focus groups are involved in the creation of popular music, you get made-for-TV boy-bands, gutless hip-hop and formulaic, downright pandering country music. We should invite and encourage feedback from our congregations but should avoid forming advisory boards or focus groups that have any say in artistic expression. The issue here is that when we do form these groups, it is implied their feedback will be implemented. Feelings will be hurt if they generate feedback you choose not to act on. This places you and your worship leadership team in a precarious position.

Essentially, when you form these groups, you have relinquished creative leadership. It is unrealistic to expect a focus group to be comprised of persons with the skills and talents necessary to guide the artistic direction of your worship ministry. As worship leaders, we have a responsibility to apply a healthy tension with our song selections, messages and liturgies. This tension moves us forward, increases our relevance and is necessary in order to remain contemporary. Focus groups function to provide feedback that would move us away from applying this tension, moving us toward choices that have more mass appeal, are less risky and ultimately limit our creativity.

Section 20

Celebrating Major Events on the Liturgical Calendar

1. Big Brass for Big Liturgical Events

2. Advent/Christmas

3. All Saints Day

4. Easter

5. Youth-Led Sundays

6. Unplugged Sundays

1. Big Brass for Big Liturgical Events

Most congregations have hidden gems. Because so many young folks (and some older folks) have skill at playing wind instruments but few opportunities to play them, it is possible to pull together a group that can help lead and accentuate music on important liturgical Sundays. Easter, All Saints, Christmas – these services are special and having a big band in addition to your other contemporary musicians can drive home the joyful and triumphant feeling each of these services usually aim to procure. Guitars, drums, keys, with a wind section creates a massive sound that leaves us no choice but to celebrate.

To get started with this idea, try to find someone who plays trumpet, who can also lead other wind instruments. Ideally, your wind section will function as a separate unit, with separate practices, and separate events. If you are lucky, you may already have a brass band for your traditional service. If so, invite them to join you. Odds are they will be thrilled to participate.

2. Advent/Christmas

While I was working on my M.Div., I developed a strong preference for the NRSV translation of the Bible. It is my go-to translation whenever I'm doing a Bible study, preparing a sermon or just reading on my own. At Christmas time, however, I especially enjoy the literary quality of the King James Version of Luke's Gospel. I like to connect to my own history, which subconsciously assigns the old English language of the King James version a higher degree of reverence, at least for that moment.

The reason I mention this is a similar phenomenon happens during the holidays in denominational churches that have both traditional and contemporary worship services. During the holidays, we see that even contemporary worshipers seek out more traditional sounds and liturgies. I've heard one person say, "I love contemporary worship, but at Christmas time I need to connect with my roots." Now I wish I were a strong enough person to have not taken that comment personally, but as the director of contemporary worship, it kind of hurt. I got over it. I used that comment to fuel a new commitment to making sure the contemporary worship we offered at Christmas time would not only be lively and relevant, reflecting current modes of worship, but also do an excellent job of connecting congregants to our shared Christian lineage.

In living out this commitment, I learned a few Do's and Don'ts.

Do – use familiar carols with a range of voice leadership allowing the entire congregation to easily sing along.

Don't – use alternate versions of familiar Christmas carols that are in different keys or in arrangements that are distant departures from their otherwise familiar melodies.

Do – go beyond music to offer visual elements. Liturgical dance and drama, along with creative liturgies, perhaps with congregational responses, tend to be more engaging to everyone.

Don't – forget to dance with the one who brought you. Keep it contemporary by using inventive instrumentation and keep it lively by incorporating a good number of guest instrumentalists and vocalists.

Do – use an array of acoustic instruments. This may be a reflection of this particular moment in time, but acoustic instruments are ideal at Christmas. Acoustic guitars, violins, cellos, upright basses, pianos, flutes are all terrific for leading Christmas worship. Acoustic instruments have the irreplaceable quality of lessening the divide between congregations and musicians. Acoustic instrumentation builds a more earthy, comfortable and intimate feel so it is ideal for the Christmas season. Drums are acoustic instruments and may be necessary for your arrangements. When it comes to percussion, however, I would encourage you not to use a full drum kit. Jingle bells are terrific. They add an immediate holiday flavor to any song. Congas, djembes and cajons do a wonderful job of accenting pieces without overpowering them.

Don't – use electric guitars. The electric sound is terrific, but on Christmas I would encourage you to consider using all acoustic instruments. With the exception of songs like "O Come, O Come Emmanuel," which lends itself to a heavy metal sound by being written in E minor, heavily distorted electric guitars are out of place in Christmas carols. Unless you are in the Transiberian Orchestra, heavy electric tones will probably disrupt the sound you are going for with Christmas carols.

Do – use the pipe organ if you've got one.

Don't – fake a pipe organ sound with a synthesizer.

Do – consider my advice on the subject and see if it helps you.

Don't – accept anything that I have to say as law. My advice here is coming from my personal experience, and its success has been guided by its context.

Holidays are special. For many of us, our memories of holidays are forged in large part from our experiences at church. The families in our congregations trust worship leaders to help make holidays memorable. At Christmas, using new music in addition to familiar carols can help start new traditions while celebrating our heritage. With classic Christmas carols, the melodies, time signatures, as well as the words for these songs are somewhat untouchable. I wouldn't mess too much with Christmas carols except for some creative instrumentation and harmonies.

For example, one year we decided to do a different version of the carol "Do you hear what I hear?" Several of us were interested in a cappella groups like Pentatonix, so we decided to give that style a try. With a human beatbox as our rhythmic foundation, we created vocal bass lines and harmonies that undergirded the familiar lead melody for the song. We received rave reviews from the congregation and created a new tradition.

A special note to worship leaders: Remember to have fun! This is your Christmas, too. It is so easy to get caught up in the stress of pulling off imaginative, evocative, well-executed worship experiences during the holidays.

A while back, I grew to dread the holidays. It was important to me to dial back my own intensity. I had to redefine the Christmas season as an opportunity, not an urgent crisis. To do this, I started planning Christmas in July. Over the following months, I worked here and there on song ideas, collaborated with the band and developed a strategy.

The most stressful event for me used to be our Lessons and Carols service. In this service, we would forgo sermons, replacing them with Scripture verses and songs. Typically, we would offer 11 or 12 different songs. As you might imagine, this would be a Herculean effort if we tried to do it all in one week. So in July, when my church sets its calendar for the holiday season, I pushed the Lessons and Carols service as far back as I could, giving myself as many weeks as possible to work in new songs. Beginning with the first Sunday following Thanksgiving, I incorporated two Christmas carols each week, so by the time the Lessons and Carols service came around, the band had all of these songs ready to go. This minimized the amount of work we needed to do the week of Lessons and Carols. This allowed me to relax and actually enjoy the holidays, knowing we were on top of things. For the Christmas season, take the reins, be proactive and have fun!

3. All Saints Day

For All Saints Sunday, you have an opportunity to help your congregation grieve the loss of loved ones as well as celebrate the gift of eternal life. In the congregations I have served on All Saints Sunday, we normally begin with songs that are quieter, more contemplative, allowing for a time of grieving. As the service goes on, the instrumentation increases in our songs as our focus turns from mourning toward celebration. By the end of the service, the songs reflect the joy of knowing that death is not the end.

This progression helps turn our mourning into dancing and celebrates the true intentions of All Saints Sunday. Explore classics like "When the Saints Go Marching In" or "I'll Fly Away" or "Soon and Very Soon." Putting fresh spins on these songs can make your All Saints Sunday a day to remember. And dress up. Yes, I know that contemporary worship is defined by a more casual dress code, but dressing up shows respect for the subject matter, which is mourning the loss and celebrating the lives of our loved ones who have gone before us.

4. Easter

On Easter it's time to go big. Wind sections, full choirs, and liturgical dancers all help capture the joy of and majesty of Easter morning. Personally, I consider Easter to be the most important day in the liturgical calendar. Theologically speaking, recognition of Jesus's resurrection is a prime directive of Christian worship. It's customary to place significant focus on Christmas, and it is not uncommon for churches to begin planning Christmas six months ahead of time. Easter, however, rarely receives as much attention. I recommend starting Easter planning in January. As you consider Easter Sunday, take some deliberate time to think about what resurrection means for you. Having a personal connection with the resurrection narrative can powerfully affect your song choices. Invest yourself into the process and follow God's leading as you plan to celebrate this important event in church life.

Easter Sunday is a wonderful opportunity to use your children's choir if you have one. If you have access to bagpipes, Easter morning is one of the few opportunities you'll have to use them. I like to use either bagpipes or a trumpet by themselves as an opening prelude to worship on Easter. Some of the methods you normally employ for planning worship from week to week need to be adjusted for Easter Sunday. If your congregation is like most, you can expect to have anywhere from 30 percent to 50 percent more people attend worship on Easter. Songs that may be familiar to your regulars may not be familiar to the additional folks who attend only on holidays. It may be worthwhile to take a brief time to teach songs to the congregation on Easter Sunday in order to maximize participation. Also, be intentional in explaining the liturgy, and be sure to invite everyone to come back!

5. Youth-Led Sundays

Through the conversations I've had with other worship leaders, it seems that we all have Sundays on our liturgical calendars when worship is led by youth. These same worship leaders find it easy to commiserate with me on how challenging it is to get our youth motivated and organized. These young people are not professional worship planners, so you can't just turn it over to them and expect a high level of excellence. Likewise, you can't take it over from them and expect them to be as engaged with the same sense of ownership.

It helps to take the worship service plan and break it down into smaller pieces. Depending on the number of young people, organizing teams that handle the different elements within the worship service is ideal. Help them develop a theme for worship that Sunday. Help ground them in Scripture, then have them weigh their ideas for the different elements of their worship service against that scriptural theme, and then let go. Start early and develop realistic milestones with a corresponding timeline for completion. This sounds like project management, because it is. Remember that youth pastors are not necessarily worship leaders and vice versa. If you have a youth pastor, the two of you will be powerful allies in helping the students work together for effective worship services.

6. Unplugged Sundays

As you develop your musical style and you get into a rhythm, eventually there will be some predictability as far as what your congregation can expect from your worship team. This can be a good thing, but I found it's also good to mix it up on occasion. Every now and then, offering something considerably different during worship can really invigorate and energize your experience. For example, try doing an acoustic set on occasion. If your band uses electric guitars and drums, try unplugging for a worship service. This creates a more intimate setting, lessening the disconnect from the band and the congregation. By mixing it up, we create a healthy F.O.M.O. (Fear Of Missing Out) in our congregations, inspiring better attendance.

♪♪♪

Section 21

Audiovisual – Important Odds and Ends

1. Recording

2. Recording the Channels versus Recording the Room

3. Amps

4. Projecting Videos During Songs

5. Proof Check Lyrics

1. Recording

Recording worship has become very important. Your recordings can be posted to your church website so that folks who can't make it to church can still experience worship at home or on the go. This makes your church experience more portable. As we endeavor to evangelize, having audio and video recordings allows us to share our music with people who don't experience it otherwise.

There are several software tools available for recording music. Some of these tools almost require a specialized degree in order to know how to use them. Common sound engineering programs can be rather complicated. If you have trained sound engineers volunteering for you, by all means seek their advice as to what they prefer. If you are to use sophisticated recording software for your recordings, make sure you have a constant stream of volunteers so that you're not completely dependent on the availability of just one skilled individual.

2. Recording the Channels versus Recording the Room

It seems like a simple distinction, but your choices here can have a profound impact on your recording quality, your budget and your volunteer hours. When you record from the individual channels, it is then required you do some mixing in order to have a finished product that captures your band's best sound. When recording from the channels, you have the option to studio your music, potentially giving your recordings a high production value. Recording and mixing from the channels, however, takes a considerable amount of time and an equally considerable degree of skill. If you have the volunteer resources to record, mix, and then post from your channels, then this may be your best option.

If you record the channels and don't add any ambient effects, it will most likely sound like you are singing in a tin can, which is not your true sound. Sometimes we can over-mix, making our recordings sound like we're singing in the Grand Canyon. Somewhere in between is where you want to be. Bear in mind that when your singers hear poor recordings of themselves, it will negatively affect their confidence, their motivation and their ability to sing fully.

Recording the room should be an easier process. The goal of recording the room is to capture what people hear when they come to worship on Sundays, or whatever day of the week you have worship. Recording the room versus recording from the channels require less mixing, assuming your recording devices catch the warmth, reverb and overall temperature of the room during worship.

One advantage of recording the room is that you can get the congregation's collective voice in your recordings as they sing along to your songs, which can be lovely. The main challenge of recording the room is tuning out all of the nonessential sound. The problem usually centers around the location of your microphones. If your microphones are too close to one individual in the congregation, they are going to be given an unintentional solo on your recordings. Hanging microphones from the ceiling or positioning them somewhere higher above the fray is ideal.

When placing recording microphones, pay attention as to where your system speakers are located. If your recording microphones are in the direct line from your main speakers, your recordings will likely redline. If your church is like most, you'll have to make decisions as to how to spend limited resources. When it comes to recording, money is spent on recording software and microphones. In my opinion, emphasis should be on the hardware versus the software. Good microphones can really make a difference on how your recordings turn out. Of course good software can have that effect as well, but software ages so quickly, where good microphones will last quite a while. Whether you are recording the channels or the room, good microphones will be essential to capturing your best sound.

3. Amps

If after writing this book, a sound tech from a contemporary worship service comes up to me and offers me a high-five, it will be because of this topic. Amplifiers are synonymous with a rock 'n roll band. In order for electric guitar players to get the complex sounds that they're looking for, amplifiers are necessary. Bass players have a deep need for that full, satisfying sound that only a big, loud bass amp can provide. Acoustic guitar amps can add character and fullness to your tone. It's hard to find guitar players who wouldn't prefer to hear themselves through an amplifier instead of just a dry, unaffected monitor.

Even so, amps cause a conundrum in sound management. Amplifiers take away from your audio technicians the ability to control the comprehensive sound coming through your sound system. It has been my experience there is a continual, ever-growing arms race that happens as musicians with amplifiers compete with each other so they can hear themselves. Bands that use amplifiers are just louder. What happens is the bass has to be turned up in order to hear it over the drums, then the lead guitar player turns their amp up in order to be heard. It does get out of control and worship directors will have to keep a constant tension on bandmates with blaring amps to limit their volume.

A common complaint I've heard over the years is that the band is too loud. As a musician, I understand and I'm in favor of using amplifiers. There are some caveats here, however. I would absolutely avoid using amplifiers that don't have XLR outputs. For reference, XLR outputs allow you to go straight into the PA system. Without XLR outputs or some other means of going directly into the sound system, you are forced to either mic the amplifier with a freestanding microphone in front of it or turn the amplifier up loud enough to fill the room.

Either of these scenarios are less than ideal. If you turn your amps up loud enough to be heard in the room, it's highly unlikely the sound will be balanced. One side will get more of a particular instrument than the other. Also, if you mic your amplifiers with a freestanding microphone, you will inevitably pick up other sounds like drums. Hooking the amplifiers directly to your sound system, however, allows you to balance the sound coming out of the amplifier and send it back through your monitors. This approach allows you to turn the amplifiers way down so that only the musicians playing through them can hear them, giving more control of your comprehensive sound back to your sound techs.

4. Projecting Videos During Songs

Depending on your multimedia capacity, it is possible to project videos during your songs. The videos play in the background with the lyrics projected over top of them. For example, we really liked the music video for Dave Matthews' song "Everyday,"[58] which shows a man going through his day hugging strangers. Since we were performing that song in worship, we decided to have the video for the song run behind the words on our multimedia screens. On another occasion we performed the song "Move" by MercyMe, and behind the words on our screens we had videos of people walking, running, dancing, moving. These were really fun ideas, but they were met with mixed reviews. Most of the people at my church I talked with after using videos during songs concluded it was really fun and engaging. A few people, however, found the videos to be a distraction. One person even found it offensive.

Because of the mixed reviews, we used the videos sparingly and only during musical offerings. If you have the capacity to project videos behind words during worship, you may want to try it to see how it goes. Your people may love it, or they may hate it. As a worship leader, just know that sometimes you have to experiment before you know if it's going to work. Projecting videos during songs captures our attention differently, allowing to connect to song not only by what we hear, but what we see. I suspect more of us will be using this idea in the years to come.

5. Proof Check Lyrics

The lyrics to your songs will either be printed in the bulletin, projected on the screen or available in some other way. It is prudent to have a procedure in place that verifies the lyrics prior to Sunday morning or whenever your services are held. A practical way to do this is to have a mock bulletin ready before you meet for practice. If your audiovisual personnel could be present while you practice, you can correct any lyrical changes on the spot so that everything is ready for worship. It has been my experience that lyric changes are necessary most weeks. Typically, denominational churches rely on administrative staff to prepare bulletins. These folks work with deadlines and juggle multiple responsibilities. Their work is important, and we show them respect by providing our song selections to them way ahead of time. Make sure to get any changes to the lyrics and song selections to them in a timely manner.

Section 22

Reclaiming the "E" Word

1. Music as Evangelism

2. Portability

3. Off-Campus Events

3. New Members — Increasing Retention

1. Music as Evangelism

Question: You have just been evangelized. What happened? Was it a good experience? Was it a bad experience? If it was a good experience, why? And if it was a bad experience, why?

Answers to these questions can inform our strategies for evangelism. When you decide you want to be more effective in sharing the Good News, your team should get together and ask these questions. If we had good experiences from being evangelized, write down single words that describe that good experience. Also imagine what it would be like to have a bad experience, and then write down the words describing that experience. The result of this exercise should be two lists: one describing a good experience with evangelism, the other describing bad experiences. These lists function as excellent criteria we can use in choosing songs.

Let's say your answer to the question, "You've just been evangelized. What happened?" Is it that you were made to feel valuable, wanted, loved, and welcomed? In this case, we should choose songs that help build on this sense of belonging and build on the awareness that God loves us and wants us to be in relationship. Using this list as a guide, we can choose songs that reinforce a person's initial decision to follow Jesus, helping listeners grow in faith.

But what if our answer to the question, "You've just been evangelized, what happened?" reflects a negative experience? For example, what if our answer to that question is "I felt judged, guilty, unworthy, inferior, shameful?" These words also help guide us in our song selections. If these words describe a negative experience of evangelism, they also could describe the way we feel when we hear songs that use similar language and inspire similar sentiment. If a song makes people feel guilty or ashamed, it is bad evangelism. If it makes you feel loved, welcomed and assured, it's good evangelism.

Remember: the bully pulpit is no good for anyone. We should make sure we don't condemn, shame, belittle, berate or browbeat with our songs. Instead, if we intend to evangelize, we need to pick songs that inspire us to feel welcome, reassured, loved and worthy.

As we endeavor to reach the unchurched or the church alumni, we should expect that these folks often carry experiences of being cast out or marginalized.[59] Choosing songs reflecting Jesus' compassion for folks who feel left out or pushed aside can go beyond just words. These songs communicate your congregation's passion to live out Jesus' mandate to seek out and serve the lost and forgotten. As you choose songs, think about how someone who is on the outside might hear and receive the song. Through the songs you choose each week, you have opportunities to extend the message of grace to someone who might feel forsaken.

2. Portability

Contemporary worship music can be very portable. This is especially advantageous when you want to use music in community service events. Music can powerfully engage a group of people in ways words alone cannot. If your church is involved at soup kitchens, urban ministries, mission trips, or similar community service events, having a portable source of music can be very valuable.

For example, at my church we decided to fund and staff the Friday morning breakfast at our local Urban Ministry Center. It was customary for the churches sponsoring these meals to give a brief devotional message to the guests once everyone was gathered. One time, I was asked to give the message at this meal, and I chose to play a song instead. After that, music became a preference for the volunteers and the guests. We found that music could reach the guests at our local Urban Ministry in dynamic and perpetual ways.

Another ministry that benefits from portability is called 16 Cents Ministries based in Greensboro, NC.[60] They offer meals and worship services under one of the major bridges downtown, where a good number of homeless people congregate for shelter. During these events, music has become paramount to worship. When we play under the bridge, the music rings through downtown, drawing people to come to share in the fellowship and the meal we have prepared.

Give some thought to how you can get your band out in the community. If you are setting up contemporary worship for the first time, and you are buying equipment for worship, consider whether or not you intend to leave the building with your worship team and then choose equipment that will best enable your intentions for ministry. If you don't have a PA system, you may want to consider one that can travel. If your congregation is committed to evangelistic enterprises, having a contemporary band that can play on location will work miracles in living out your mission.

Portable contemporary worship can open up a host of new possibilities. An idea I've always wanted to try, but have yet to carve out time for, is to have of a lawn-chair church. The idea is to use social media resources like meet-up groups to announce and coordinate a group of people to meet at a public park, bring lawn chairs, perhaps some food to share, and a heart for worship. Then show up with guitars, djembes, cajons, flutes, accordions, and so forth and a scriptural focus with a brief message. Then see what happens. I like the idea of not meeting in the same place twice in a row. This, of course, is all predicated on the portability of contemporary worship music. What is great about this idea is that it can happen pretty much any day and time people can agree on. Explore this idea. Talk about it and see what other ideas come up from being able to go mobile with your worship.

3. Off-Campus Events

When we take our worship off site, we give ourselves the opportunity to become more unified as a group. Often, disagreements and divisions that exist inside church walls seem to disappear when the church is represented out in the community. By setting up events off-campus, we come together under a common identity. There may be large community functions where your group can set up with a full PA system and all the bells and whistles. If such opportunities can be created, I would certainly suggest participating in them. You can create your own events as well. For example, bringing music to retirement communities is a wonderful way of serving our wiser generations. It's relatively easy to set this up. It doesn't require much instrumentation, a guitar or two, perhaps an in-house piano, a few singers, and you're off and running.

Speaking of running: 5Ks, marathons, and other races usually benefit from having live music. If you have a portable band, offer your talents for these events, especially when their function is to raise money and awareness for good causes. Taking a guitar and some singers along with you for hospital visitation is usually appreciated. And let your pastors know of your availability to assist with weddings and funerals. I've had the remarkable joy of playing at both weddings and funerals. I suspect your group will cherish the opportunity to participate in these sacred moments, which remind us of the importance of music. In turn, participating in these events helps build our own sense of value and identity as musicians.

4. New Members — Increasing Retention

When new members visit your worship services, the specific experiences you create can significantly affect whether they return. Turning visitors into members usually comes down to how they are greeted, what follow up takes place, and how they are then connected with your congregation. Modern worshippers have adopted a consumer mentality, making it harder to attract and retain new people.

It is common sense to greet and welcome new visitors and make sure any information they need is readily available. During worship, clear instructions will help keep visitors from feeling lost. In contemporary worship, using the projection screens to display congregational responses works well to ease anxieties about not being on the same page (literally) as everyone else.

As for ice breakers with visitors, remember that food helps start conversations. For example, in our contemporary services, we have a group of volunteers who bring food for the band and AV crew each Sunday. There always seems to be more than we can eat. After services, I would go around and offer those extra goodies to the folks who were hanging around. This functions as a terrific icebreaker for introducing myself to new members. Great conversations can get started over Krispy Kreme doughnuts, gorilla bread and breakfast pizza. And remember that new member retention is everyone's job, so encourage your worship teams to introduce themselves to new people when they can.

To help visitors feel more comfortable in approaching your group, make sure all of the volunteers have name badges. In music ministry, it is rare that weeks go by without visitors coming up to us after worship to tell us how much they liked the music. These are great opportunities to connect with potential new members. Let these folks know how much you value their presence and their feedback. Encourage them to visit again. Those five or ten minutes after worship are vital in the process of someone deciding to return.

As a band, avoid sticking to your own clique, but instead challenge yourselves to go out into the congregation and meet someone new each week.

Final Thoughts: Postlude

Recently, I was watching a friend of mine weld a new threshold at the entry way to our church parking lot. This metal threshold is designed to cover electrical wires that would otherwise be driven over by hundreds of cars. My church was doing a massive live nativity for the first time, and we were working out the logistics as we went along. I talked to him for a moment, and he explained how he was glad to be able to contribute. He said he is honored to literally help build a foundation that others can build on in the future. "I can't play music, I can't preach, but I can weld," he said. Then I watched him cut metal with fire.

When we work to offer contemporary worship, we have a similar hope — to set a foundation on which future generations can build. Our job is to move forward in faith, using our specific gifts in recognition that we are all part of the Body of Christ. We strive for excellence as we seek to honor God through our work. We hope to take our worship to new, more enriching levels. We pray we succeed in telling God's story in new ways to new people, providing new opportunities for God's truth to permeate our being. When we start contemporary worship in our churches, we hope to reinvent and reorient ourselves, so that we can further animate the Gospel as we live out our commissioning to share the God News.

This book is my way of "welding a threshold."

I am aware that this book has somewhat of an identity crisis between academic and practical topics. I considered writing two books from these different vantage points. One book would come from an academic stance, attempting to inform contemporary worship from a meta-narrative perspective. The other book would be more of a how-to manual, a "Contemporary Worship for Dummies." I decided that both were necessary for anyone who has the responsibility of implementing contemporary worship. I concluded that knowing why we do contemporary worship is just as important as how we do it.

History and theology matter to our understanding of contemporary worship, and they shape its future. Contemporary worship does not happen in a classroom, however. It happens in a real world, filled with real people and real challenges. Providing a resource that informs both the theoretical premises as well as the practical realities of contemporary worship is a worthy endeavor, and I pray that this book accomplishes this task.

Please I am praying for you. Be bold; be adventurous. Embrace your gifts and share them. Add to this foundation and build upon it. Employ your Faith, Hope and Love into your ministry and carry us forward.

May the Grace and Peace of our Lord Jesus Christ go with you now and always.

Endnotes

Preface:
1. "Frames" Online Seminar Hosted by the Barna Group," accessed January 29, 2014 from 10:00 AM to 3:00 PM (PST), http://barnaframes.com/frameslive.

Introduction:
2. Rory Noland, *The Heart of the Artist* (Grand Rapids: Zondervan, 1999).

Section 1: What is Contemporary Worship?
3. "The Twelfth Night, Act I, Scene I," William Shakespeare, accessed October 10, 2014, http://shakespeare.mit.edu/twelfth_night/full.html/.
4. Don E. Saliers, *Music and Theology* (Nashville, TN: Abingdon Press, 2007), 9.
5. "The Confessions IX," Church Fathers," accessed September 25, 2014, http://www.newadvent.org/fathers/110109.htm, Chapter 6.
6. Saliers, *Music and Theology*, 22.
7. Jeremy Begbie, *Theology, Music, and Time* (Cambridge: Cambridge University Press, 2000), 14-15.
8. Begbie, *Theology, Music, and Time*, 273.
9. Saliers, *Music and Theology*, 24.
10. Lisa M. Hess, *Learning in a Musical Key: Insight for Theology in Performance Mode* (Eugene, OR: Pickwick Publications, 2011), 61.
11. Begbie, *Theology, Music, and Time*, 179.

Section 2: Contemporary Worship: Are We There Yet?
12. "Who are the Congregationalists?" Congressional Library and Archives, accessed April 27, 2015, http://www.congregationallibrary.org/about/congregational-christian
13. Leonard, Bill interview by author, Winston-Salem, NC, October 23, 2013.
14. Saliers, *Music and Theology*, 17, 56, 59.
15. Maria Boulding, trans., *The Confessions by Saint Augustine* (New York: New City Press, 1997), 181.
16. Boulding, *The Confessions by Saint Augustine*, 180.
17. Don H. Compier, *Listening to Popular Music* (Minneapolis, MN: Fortress Press, 2013) 52.
18. Compier, *Listening to Popular Music*, 54.
19. Saliers, Music and Theology, 56.
20. Piere Weiss and Richard Taruskin, *Music in the Western World: A History of Documents* (London: Macmillan), 62.

21. Albert L. Blackwell, *The Sacred in Music* (Louisville: Westminster John Knox Press, 1999) 129.
22. Jean Calvin, *Institutes of the Christian Religion* (London: J. Clarke, 1949) 499.
23. Calvin, 1509-1564. *Theological Treatises* (Philadelphia: Westminister Press, 1954) 53-54.
24. Compier, *Listening to Popular Music*, 72.
25. Quoted in Roland Bainton, *Here I Stand: A Life of Martin Luther* (New York: New American Library, 1950) 266-267.
26. Compier, *Listening to Popular Music*, 73-76.
27. Samuel M Jackson, Editor, *Ulrich Zwingli: Early Writings* (Durham, NC: Labyrnith Press),56.
28. Compier, Listening to Popular Music, 64-68.
29. Bill Leonard, interview by author, Winston-Salem, NC, October 23, 2013
30. Adam Hamilton, *Revival: Faith as Wesley Lived It* (Nashville: Abingdon Press, 2014), 130.
31. "*Motu Proprio*, Pope Pius X", http://www. americancatholicpress.org/articlesMotuProprio.html , accessed - September 19, 2015.
32. "*Motu Proprio*, Pope Pius X," http://www. americancatholicpress.org/articlesMotuProprio.html , accessed - September 19, 2015.
33. "Pope Pius X Writings: *Motu Proprio* in 1903" http://www. adoremus.org/MotuProprio.html, accessed September 19, 2015. The numbered item (19) is missing form the American Catholic Press website.
34. "*Motu Proprio*, Pope Pius X," http://www. americancatholicpress.org/articlesMotuProprio.html , accessed - September 19, 2015
35. Begbie, Theology, Music, and Time, 13
36. Geoffrey Hayden, *John Tavener: Glimpses of Paradise*, (London: Gollancz, 1995), 209.
37. Leonard, interview by author, Winston-Salem, NC, October 23, 2013

Section 3: Sticking with Traditional

38. Kelly Fryer, *Reclaiming the "C" Word: Daring to be Church Again* (Minneapolis, Augsburg Fortress, 2006). 69.
39. Leonard, interview by author, Winston-Salem, NC, October 23, 2013
40. "American churches: A failure to thrive?" https://baptistnews. com/opinion/item/7879-american-churches-a-failure-to-thrive, accessed November 17, 2013.
41. Leonard, interview by author, Winston-Salem, NC, October 23, 2013

42. Leonard, interview by author, Winston-Salem, NC, October 23, 2013

Section 4: Ch- Ch- Ch- Changes
43. Paul Tillich, "The Church and Contemporary Culture," World Christian Education - Second Quarter (1956): 41-43.
44. Michael J. Gilmour, *Gods and Guitars: Seeking the Sacred in Post-1960s Popular Music* (Baylor University Press, 2009).
45. Guy L. Beck, *Sacred Sound: Experiencing Music and World Religions* (Waterloo, Ont.: Wilfrid Laurier University Press, 2006), 85.
46. Beck, *Sacred Sound*, 85.

Section 5: Getting Started
47. Begbie, interviewed by author, Durham, NC, March 5, 2014.
48. Jill Crainshaw, interviewed by author, Winston-Salem, NC, October 30, 2013

Section 9: Sacred Space
49. Medical Mission Immersion trip to Nicaragua, Wake Forest University, April 17, 2008.

Section 10: Contemporary Liturgy
50. Carol Kelly-Gangi, Editor, *Mother Teresa: Her Essential Wisdom* (New York: Fall River Press, 2006) 51.
51. "Salvage Garden," accessed October 19, 2015, http://salvagegarden.org/.

Section 12: Musical Diversity
52. Peter Menconi, *The Intergenerational Church: Understanding Congregations from WWII to www.com* (Littleton, CO: Mt. Sage Publishing, 2010) 173.
53. Marcus J. Borg, *The Heart of Christianity: Rediscovering a Life of Faith.* First edition (San Francisco: HarperSanFrancisco, 2003) 12.

Section 14: Song Planning
54. Begbie, *Theology Music and Time*, 105.

Section 16: Considerations When Choosing Songs
55. Margaret Kornfeld, *Cultivating Wholeness: A Guide to Care and Counseling in Faith Communities* (New York: Continuum, 2001).

Section 17: People and Processes
56. Noland, *Heart of the Artist*, 115-147.

Section 18: Conflict Management
57. Peter Titelman, *Triangles: Bowen Family Systems Theory Perspectives.* (Green Bay, WI: Routledge Ltd, 2008) 5

Section 21: Audiovisual — Odds and Ends

58. "Everyday, by Dave Matthews Band," accessed on October 19, 2015

Section 22: Reclaiming the "E" Word

59. Borg, *The Heart of Christianity: Rediscovering a Life of Faith.* First edition. (San Francisco: HarperSanFrancisco, 2003) 12-13
60. "16 Cents Ministries," accessed October 19, 2015, http://www.16centsministry.org

Author Brian Thomas Russell

Brian is currently serving as Director of Contemporary Worship and Creative Arts at Memorial United Methodist Church in Thomasville, North Carolina. He is also the Director of the Arts Alive Art Academy. Brian's tenure in leading contemporary worship spans two decades in a variety of denominational settings including Catholic, Baptist, Lutheran, Moravian, AME Zion, United Methodist and nondenominational churches.

A 1990 graduate of Belmont Abbey College in North Carolina with a major in sociology, Brian completed his Master of Divinity from Wake Forest University in 2011. While at Wake Forest, Brian also earned the Graduate Certificate in Spirituality and Health awarded by the School of Divinity and the School of Medicine.

Brian is a founding member of Salvage Garden – a 501(c)(3) organization commissioned to serve the spiritual growth of persons with exceptional challenges.

In 2014, Brian began working as a consultant with churches that are making efforts to start or reinvent contemporary worship.

— To Order —

The Complete Contemporary Worship Handbook
How to Build and Sustain Meaningful Worship
in Modern Denominational Churches
by Brian T. Russell

You may order this book from the publisher

LangMarc Publishing
P.O. Box 90488
Austin, Texas 78709-0488
phone: 512-394-0989
www.langmarc.com
e-mail: langmarc@booksails.com

Call or e-mail for store, workshop or quantity discounts.
Check website www.langmarc.com
for occasional online specials
Also available on Amazon.com

U.S.A. — $19.95+ $3 shipping
(shipping for multiple copies will be at cost)
Texas residents add 8.25% sales tax
Canada — $23 + $5 shipping

Name:_____

Street:_____

City, State, Zip:_____

Phone Number:_____

Number of books:_____

Total Cost:_____

Check or Credit Card Number:_____

Expiration Date:_____

CPSIA information can be obtained
at www.ICGtesting.com
Printed in the USA
BVOW06s0830221117
501085BV00011B/81/P